GREED *is* IDOLATRY

Does it matter?

RICHARD S. HOCKETT

GREED IS IDOLATRY
Does it matter?
by Richard S. Hockett

Printed in the United States of America

ISBN 9781498404280

www.xulonpress.com

Other books by Richard S. Hockett

Foundations of Wisdom: The Book of Proverbs,
Xulon Press, 2009

Choose the Best! The "Better Thans" of Wisdom,
Xulon Press, 2013

Parenting with Proverbs: A Workbook for Families,
Xulon Press, 2013

The Spiritual Wisdom and Understanding of Colossians,
Xulon Press, 2014

TABLE OF CONTENTS

PREFACE

In my late 30's I was asked by the elders in the church we were attending to teach a nine-month Old Testament survey to an adult class of about 40-50 seniors twice my age.

One of the results was a profound effect on me as I saw the parallels of Israel's idolatry and the Church's greed. (The New Testament calls greed idolatry.) The effect was overwhelming. I organized what I was seeing into a detailed outline in order to prepare a course on the subject, but never taught it.

Over the last couple decades I continued to see this parallel. When I retired recently I believed I was to write a book based upon that outline. This is the result. I still find it overwhelming. But God's truth is good, and His love for his Church is redeeming.

May this book do whatever God desires.

Richard Hockett, San Jose, CA

INTRODUCTION

The purpose of this book is to compare and contrast the idolatry of God's Wife, Israel, under the Old Covenant with the greed (which is idolatry) of the Son's Bride, the Church, under the New Covenant. The idolatry of the nation Israel (from Jacob to the diaspora by Babylon) occurred over about 1,700 years and had consequences for God's Wife. The greed of the Church has occurred for over 2,000 years and has had consequences for the Son's Bride – those consequences continue even today.

To compare the two may seem confusing at first. What does idolatry, which is an act with man-made physical idols, have to do with greed, which is a desire? The answer comes from understanding how the Old Covenant and the New Covenant relate to each other. The Old Covenant relates mostly to the physical. The New Covenant relates mostly to the non-physical.

For example, under the Old Covenant with Israel, the Law of God was written on tablets of stone. Under the New Covenant with the Church, the Law of God is written on hearts and minds by the Spirit. Under the Old Covenant, adultery was the physical sexual union with another man's wife. Under the New Covenant, the inner desire to have physical sexual union with another man's wife is adultery. Under the Old Covenant, murder is the taking of another's life. Under the New Covenant, the inner desire to take another man's life is murder.

Under the Old Covenant, idolatry was the worship and service to physical idols. Under the New Covenant, the worship and serving of money is an inner excessive desire to have more, which is called greed. Under the Old Covenant, the idolatry of God's people provoked God's jealous wrath in the form of physical judgment. Under the New Covenant, the greed of God's people provokes God's jealous wrath in the form of spiritual opposition.

Two greatest commandments	**Opposite under the Old Covenant**	**Opposite under the New Covenant**
Love the Lord your God with all your heart and with all your soul and with all your mind.	Physical idolatry. *You shall not make for yourself an idol in the form of anything in heaven above or on the earth beneath or in the waters below. You shall not bow down to them or worship them.* The book of *Hosea* illustrates this graphically.	Loving something other than the Lord your God; includes greed which is idolatry.
Love your neighbor as yourself.	Oppression (obtain gain for ourselves at the expense of, or loss to, our neighbor). The book of *Amos* illustrates this graphically.	Oppression (loving ourselves at the expense of our neighbor; withholding servant-hood to our neighbor)

Why is this important today?

In *Matthew 22:34-40* Jesus revealed that all the Law and the Prophets hang on two commandments: (1) *Love the Lord your God with all your heart and with all your soul and with all your mind*, and (2) *Love your neighbor as yourself.*

> *Matthew 22:34-40*
> ***34** Hearing that Jesus had silenced the Sadducees, the Pharisees got together. **35** One of them, an expert in the law, tested him with this question: **36** "Teacher, which is the greatest commandment in the Law?" **37** Jesus replied: "Love the Lord your God with all your heart and with all your soul and with all your mind. **38** This is the first and greatest commandment. **39** And the second is like it: 'Love your neighbor as yourself.' **40** All the Law and the Prophets hang on these two commandments."*

This revelation of the fundamental relationship between the Old Testament Law and Prophets to these specific two commandments on love, neither of which is in the Ten Commandments given to Moses, is actually revolutionary and astounding.

I suggest there is a corollary concerning the opposite of these two commandments.

Old Covenant	**New Covenant**
Law written on stone *Exodus 24:14*	Law written on hearts and minds (inner) by the Spirit *Jeremiah 31:33; Hebrews 8:7-12; 10:15-17*
Adultery *Exodus 20:14*	Lust (an inner desire to have another man's wife sexually) *Matthew 5:27-28*
Murder *Exodus 20:13*	Anger (an inner desire to end another man's life) *Matthew 5:27-28*
Idolatry Exodus *20:4*	Greed (an inner excessive desire to have more) *Colossians 3:5; Ephesians 5:5; Matthew 6:24*
God's jealous wrath *Exodus 20:5*	God's jealous wrath (inner opposition) *James 4:1-6; Ephesians 5:6; Colossians 3:6*

The opposite of "*Love the Lord your God with all your heart and with all your soul and with all your mind*'" is something called idolatry. *Exodus* 20:3-6 shows a contrast between making an idol, bowing down to it or worshipping it, and giving what is due the LORD (*no other gods* ***before me***).

> *Exodus 20:3-6*
> ***3*** *"You shall have no other gods before me.* ***4*** *"You*
> *shall not make for yourself an idol in the form of*
> *anything in heaven above or on the earth beneath*
> *or in the waters below.* ***5*** *You shall not bow down*
> *to them or worship them; for I, the LORD your*
> *God, am a jealous God, punishing the children*
> *for the sin of the fathers to the third and fourth*
> *generation of those who hate me,* ***6*** *but showing*
> *love to a thousand generations of those who love*
> *me and keep my commandments.*

The opposite of "*Love your neighbor as yourself*" is something that I will sum up in the word oppression. Under the New Covenant, love of our neighbor is revealed by Jesus' example: to bring gain to us at his expense (*1 Peter 2:24; 2 Corinthians 8:9; 1 John 3:16*). Oppression is the opposite: to obtain gain for ourselves at the expense of, or loss to, our neighbor.

1 Peter 2:24
24 *He himself bore our sins in His body on the tree, so that we might die to sins and live for righteousness; by His wounds you have been healed.*

2 Corinthians 8:9
9 *For you know the grace of our Lord Jesus Christ, that though He was rich, yet for your sakes He became poor, so that you through His poverty might become rich.*

1 John 3:16
***16** This is how we know what love is: Jesus Christ laid down His life for us. And we ought to lay down our lives for our brothers.*

We know from Scripture that there is a key relationship between the two commandments. The first demands the second: "*Whoever loves God must also love his brother.*" (*I John 4:21*) I suggest there is also a key relationship between idolatry and oppression. This is inferred, for example, by *1 John 4:20* which says, *If anyone says, "I love God," yet hates his brother, he is a liar.* So, if I am hating my brother (i.e., oppressing him), I cannot claim to be loving God, and therefore I must be doing the opposite somewhere in my life (i.e., idolatry).

Why might it be important to understand what the Scriptures teach about idolatry, since most of us Christians have no carved images or cast idols that we worship or bow down to?

The reason is that in the New Testament we find that greed is idolatry (*Colossians 3:5; Ephesians 5:6)* and that there are many kinds of greed (*Luke 12:15)*.

Colossians 3:5
***5** Put to death, therefore, whatever belongs to your earthly nature: sexual immorality, impurity, lust, evil desires and greed, which is idolatry.*

Ephesians 5:5
***5** For of this you can be sure: No immoral, impure or greedy person--such a man is an idolater--has any inheritance in the kingdom of Christ and of God.*

Luke 12:13-15
***13** Someone in the crowd said to him, "Teacher, tell my brother to divide the inheritance with me." **14** Jesus replied, "Man, who appointed me a judge or an arbiter between you?" **15** Then he said to them, "Watch out! Be on your guard against all kinds of greed; a man's life does not consist in the abundance of his possessions."*

We will spend some time trying to understand what greed is, and find out that greed is widespread. Not only that, but greed has been widespread since the early church. This is not a new phenomenon.

In this book we will seek to understand what idolatry was in the Old Testament, and how greed is related to idolatry for us. The New Testament reveals that the Old Testament Scriptures are *useful for our teaching, rebuking, correcting and training in righteousness, so that we can be thoroughly equipped for every good work (2 Timothy 3:15-16). 2 Peter 1:16-21* indicates we (the church) should pay attention to the word of the prophets (in the context the OT prophets).

If we look at the pattern and characteristics of idolatry and its consequences in the OT, and then ask ourselves how these manifest themselves under the New Covenant concerning greed, what can we see about ourselves? We will look at how the pattern for idolatry among God's people in the Old Testament gives us insight into the pattern from greed among God's people today.

We will look at:

- What idolatry was in the Old Testament and what greed is in the New Testament.
- What happens to those who have idols and what happens to those who have greed.

- The tenacity of idolatry through generations and the tenacity of greed through generations.
- The influences for idolatry and the influences for greed.
- How Israel became worse in idolatry than the surrounding nations, and how the church has become worse in greed than Sodom, Israel and Judah.
- How God responded to idolatry in his people in the Old Testament, and how He responds to greed in His people in the New Testament.

IDOLATRY

In this chapter we will look at idolatry and related concepts as listed below. The Old Testament has a great deal to say about this subject.

- Idolatry and idols
- Idols were manufactured by humans and worshipped
- Some examples of idols that were worshipped
- Sacrifices were made to the idols
- There is a relationship between idols and demons
- Idolatry is an act of the sinful nature (New Testament)
- Some of the gods were given names
- One could make a covenant with a god
- The relationship between God's people and idols, or gods, is often called prostitution, unfaithful, or adulterous
- Other relationships with idols or gods included looking to them for guidance, fearing them, and trusting in them

IDOLATRY and IDOLS

We have suggested that idolatry in a broad sense was the opposite of *Love the Lord your God with all your heart and with all your soul and with all your mind. Exodus 20:3-6* shows a contrast between making an idol, bowing down to it or worshipping it, and giving what is due the LORD (*no other gods* ***before me***).

Exodus 20:3-6
3 *"You shall have no other gods before me.* ***4*** *"You shall not make for yourself an idol in the form of anything in heaven above or on the earth beneath or in the waters below.* ***5*** *You shall not bow down to them or worship them; for I, the LORD your God, am a jealous God, punishing the children for the sin of the fathers to the third and fourth generation of those who hate me,* ***6*** *but showing love to a thousand generations of those who love me and keep my commandments.*

Idolatry was the displacing of what is due the Lord alone with something humans made for humans (*make for yourselves)* that humans subjugated themselves to (*bowed down to)* or revered as greater than themselves in some sense (*worshipped.*) The idols were made in forms from three realms (*in heaven*, *on the earth*, or *in the waters below*). The idols were physical objects that represented gods in these three realms.

IDOLS WERE MANUFACTURED BY HUMANS AND WORSHIPPED

Isaiah 44:9-19
9 *All who* ***make idols*** *are nothing, and the things they treasure are worthless. Those who would speak up for them are blind; they are ignorant, to their own shame.* ***10*** *Who* ***shapes a god and casts an idol****, which can profit him nothing?* ***11*** *He and his kind will be put to shame; craftsmen are nothing but men. Let them all come together and take their stand; they will be brought down to terror and infamy.* ***12 The blacksmith takes a tool and works with it in the coals; he shapes an idol with hammers, he forges it with the might of his arm.*** *He gets hungry and loses his strength; he drinks no water and grows faint.* ***13 The carpenter measures with a line and makes an outline with a marker; he***

roughs it out with chisels and marks it with compasses. He shapes it *in the form of man, of man in all his glory, that it may dwell in a shrine.* ***14*** *He cut down cedars, or perhaps took a cypress or oak. He let it grow among the trees of the forest, or planted a pine, and the rain made it grow.* ***15*** *It is man's fuel for burning; some of it he takes and warms himself, he kindles a fire and bakes bread. But he also* ***fashions a god*** *and* ***worships it;*** *he* ***makes an idol and bows down to it.*** ***16*** *Half of the wood he burns in the fire; over it he prepares his meal, he roasts his meat and eats his fill. He also warms himself and says, "Ah! I am warm; I see the fire."* ***17*** *From the rest* ***he makes a god, his idol; he bows down to it and worships. He prays to it and says, "Save me; you are my god." 18*** *They know nothing, they understand nothing; their eyes are plastered over so they cannot see, and their minds closed so they cannot understand.* ***19*** *No one stops to think, no one has the knowledge or understanding to say, "Half of it I used for fuel; I even baked bread over its coals, I roasted meat and I ate. Shall I make a detestable thing from what is left? Shall I bow down to a block of wood?"*

Habakkuk 2:18-19

18 *"Of what value is an idol, since a* ***man has carved it****? Or an image that teaches lies? For* ***he who makes it trusts in his own creation****; he makes idols that cannot speak.* ***19*** *Woe to him who says to wood, 'Come to life!' Or to lifeless stone, 'Wake up!' Can it give guidance? It is covered with gold and silver; there is no breath in it. him; he cannot save himself, or say, "Is not this thing in my right hand a lie?"*

Isaiah 40:18-20

18 *To whom, then, will you compare God? What image will you compare him to?* ***19*** *As for an* ***idol, a craftsman casts it, and a goldsmith overlays it with gold and fashions silver chains for it. 20*** *A man too poor to present such an offering selects wood* *that will not rot. He looks for a skilled craftsman to* ***set up an idol that will not topple****.*

Jeremiah 10:3-9

3 *For the customs of the peoples are worthless; they cut a tree out of the forest, and* ***a craftsman shapes it with his chisel.*** *4* ***They adorn it with silver and gold; they fasten it with hammer and nails so it will not totter. 5*** *Like a scarecrow in a melon patch, their idols cannot speak; they must be carried because they cannot walk. Do not fear them; they can do no harm nor can they do any good."* ***6*** *No one is like you, O LORD; you are great, and your name is mighty in power.* ***7*** *Who should not revere you, O King of the nations? This is your due. Among all the wise men of the nations and in all their kingdoms, there is no one like you.* ***8*** *They are all senseless and foolish; they are taught by worthless wooden idols.* ***9 Hammered silver is brought from Tarshish and gold from Uphaz. What the craftsman and goldsmith have made is then dressed in blue and purple-- all made by skilled workers.***

Judges 17:1-4

1 *Now a man named Micah from the hill country of Ephraim* ***2*** *said to his mother, "The eleven hundred shekels of silver that were taken from you and about which I heard you utter a curse--I have that silver with me; I took it." Then his mother said, "The LORD bless you, my son!"* ***3*** *When he returned the eleven hundred shekels of silver to his mother, she said, "****I solemnly consecrate my silver to the LORD for my son to make a carved image and a cast idol****. I will give it back to you."* ***4*** *So he returned the silver to his mother, and she took two hundred shekels of silver and gave them to a* ***silversmith, who made them into the image and the idol****. And they were put in Micah's house.*

SOME EXAMPLES OF IDOLS THAT WERE WORSHIPPED

Judges 8:27
27 *Gideon made the gold into* ***an ephod****, which he placed in Ophrah, his town. All Israel prostituted themselves by worshiping it there, and it became a snare to Gideon and his family.*

1 Kings 12:26-30
26 *Jeroboam thought to himself, "The kingdom will now likely*
revert to the house of David. ***27*** *If these people go up to offer*
sacrifices at the temple of the LORD in Jerusalem, they will
again give their allegiance to their lord, Rehoboam king of
Judah. They will kill me and return to King Rehoboam." ***28***
After seeking advice, the king made ***two golden calves****. He said*
to the people, "It is too much for you to go up to Jerusalem. Here
are your gods, O Israel, who brought you up out of Egypt." ***29***
One he set up in Bethel, and the other in Dan. ***30*** *And this thing*
became a sin; the people went even as far as Dan to worship the
one there.

2 Chronicles 34:3-7
3 *In the eighth year of his [Josiah's] reign, while he was still*
young, he began to seek the God of his father David. In his
twelfth year he began to ***purge Judah and Jerusalem of high***
places, Asherah poles, carved idols and cast images*.* ***4*** *Under*
his direction the ***altars of the Baals*** *were torn down; he cut to*
pieces the ***incense altars*** *that were above them, and smashed*
the ***Asherah poles****, the idols and the images. These he broke*
to pieces and scattered over the graves of those who had sac-
rificed to them. ***5*** *He burned the bones of the priests on their*
altars, and so he purged Judah and Jerusalem. ***6 In the towns***
of Manasseh, Ephraim and Simeon, as far as Naphtali, and
in the ruins around them, *7* ***he tore down the altars and the***
Asherah poles and crushed the idols to powder and cut to

pieces all the incense altars throughout Israel. *Then he went back to Jerusalem.*

2 Kings 17:16

16 *They forsook all the commands of the LORD their God and made for themselves two idols cast in the shape of calves, and* ***an Asherah pole****. They* ***bowed down to all the starry hosts****, and they* ***worshipped Baal****.*

Ezekiel 8:9-16

9 *And he said to me, "Go in and see the wicked and detestable things they are doing here."* ***10*** *So I went in and looked, and I saw* ***portrayed all over the walls all kinds of crawling things and detestable animals and all the idols of the house of Israel****.*
11 *In front of them stood seventy elders of the house of Israel, and Jaazaniah son of Shaphan was standing among them. Each had a censer in his hand, and a fragrant cloud of incense was rising.* ***12*** *He said to me, "Son of man, have you seen what the elders of the house of Israel are doing in the darkness,* ***each at the shrine of his own idol?*** *They say, 'The LORD does not see us; the LORD has forsaken the land.' "* ***13*** *Again, he said, "You will see them doing things that are even more detestable."*
14 *Then he brought me to the entrance to the north gate of the house of the LORD, and I saw* ***women sitting there, mourning for Tammuz.*** ***15*** *He said to me, "Do you see this, son of man? You will see things that are even more detestable than this."*
16 *He then brought me into the inner court of the house of the LORD, and there at the entrance to the temple, between the portico and the altar, were about* ***twenty-five men. With their backs toward the temple of the LORD and their faces toward the east, they were bowing down to the sun in the east.***

Ezekiel 14:1-5

1 *Some of the* ***elders of Israel*** *came to me and sat down in front of me.* ***2*** *Then the word of the LORD came to me:* ***3*** *"Son of* *man,* ***these men have set up idols in their hearts*** *and* ***put wicked stumbling blocks before their faces****. Should I let them inquire of me at all?* ***4*** *Therefore speak to them and tell them, 'This is what the Sovereign LORD says: When any Israelite sets up idols in his heart and puts a wicked stumbling block before his face and then goes to a prophet, I the LORD will answer him myself in keeping with his great idolatry.* ***5*** *I will do this to recapture the hearts of the people of Israel, who have all deserted me for their idols.'*

Zephaniah 1:5
5 *those who bow down on the roofs to* ***worship the starry host****, those who bow down and swear by the LORD and who also swear by* ***Molech****,*

SACRIFICES WERE MADE TO THE IDOLS

Isaiah 57:3-10
3 *"But you--come here, you sons of a sorceress, you offspring of adulterers and prostitutes!* ***4*** *Whom are you mocking? At whom do you sneer and stick out your tongue? Are you not a brood of rebels, the offspring of liars?* ***5*** *You burn with lust among the oaks and under every spreading tree;* ***you sacrifice your children in the ravines and under the overhanging crags****.* ***6***
[The idols] among the smooth stones of the ravines are your portion; they, they are your lot. Yes, to them you have poured ***out drink offerings*** *and* ***offered grain offerings****. In the light of these things, should I relent?* ***7*** *You have made your bed on a high and lofty hill; there you went up to* ***offer your sacrifices****.* ***8***
Behind your doors and your doorposts you have put your pagan symbols. Forsaking me, you uncovered your bed, you climbed into it and opened it wide; you made a pact with those whose beds you love, and you looked on their nakedness. ***9 You went to Molech with olive oil*** *and increased your perfumes. You sent your ambassadors far away; you descended to the grave itself*
! ***10*** *You were wearied by all your ways, but you would not say,*

'It is hopeless.' You found renewal of your strength, and so you did not faint.

2 Kings 17:17
***17 They sacrificed their sons and daughters in the fire**. They practiced divination and sorcery and sold themselves to do evil in the eyes of the LORD, provoking him to anger.*

THERE IS A RELATIONSHIP BETWEEN IDOLS AND DEMONS

Deuteronomy 32:16-17
***16** They made him jealous with their foreign gods and angered him with their **detestable idols**. **17 They sacrificed to demons**, which are not God-- gods they had not known, gods that recently appeared, gods your fathers did not fear.*

1 Corinthians 10:18-20
***18** Consider the people of Israel: Do not those who eat the sacrifices participate in the altar? **19** Do I mean then that a **sacrifice offered to an idol** is anything, or that an idol is anything? **20** No, but the **sacrifices of pagans are offered to demons,** not to God, and I do not want you to be participants with demons.*

IDOLATRY IS AN ACT OF THE SINFUL NATURE. (The King James Version refers to idolatry as a work of the flesh.)

Galatians 5:19-20
***19 The acts of the sinful nature are obvious**: sexual immorality, impurity and debauchery; **20 idolatry** and witchcraft; hatred, discord, jealousy, fits of rage, selfish ambition, dissensions, factions **21** and envy; drunkenness, orgies, and the like. **I** warn you, as I did before, that those who live like this will not inherit the kingdom of God.*

SOME OF THE GODS WERE GIVEN NAMES.

Judges 6:31
6 *But Joash replied to the hostile crowd* ***around*** *him, "Are you going to plead Baal's cause? Are you trying to save him? Whoever fights for him shall be put to death by morning!* ***If Baal really is a god****, he can defend himself when someone breaks down his altar."*

1 Kings 18:21
18 *Elijah went before the people and said, "How long will you waver between two opinions? If the LORD is God, follow him; but* ***if Baal is God****, follow him." But the people said nothing.*

Jeremiah 11:13
13 *You have as many gods as you have towns, O Judah; and the altars you have set up to burn incense to that* ***shameful god Baal*** *are as many as the streets of Jerusalem.'*

1 Kings 11:33
33 *I will do this because they have forsaken me and worshiped* ***Ashtoreth the goddess of the Sidonians****,* ***Chemosh the god of the Moabites****, and* ***Molech the god of the Ammonites****, and have not walked in my ways, nor done what is right in my eyes, nor kept my statutes and laws as David, Solomon's father, did.*

ONE COULD MAKE A COVENANT WITH A GOD.

Exodus 23:31-32
31 *"I will establish your borders from the Red Sea to the Sea of the Philistines, and from the desert to the River. I will hand over to you the people who live in the land and you will drive them out before you.* ***32 Do not make a covenant*** *with them or* ***with their gods****.*

THE RELATIONSHIP BETWEEN GOD'S PEOPLE AND IDOLS, OR GODS, IS OFTEN CALLED PROSTITUTION, UNFAITHFUL, OR ADLUTEROUS

Isaiah 57:1-10

1 *The righteous perish, and no one ponders it in his heart; devout men are taken away, and no one understands that the righteous are taken away to be spared from evil.* ***2*** *Those who walk uprightly enter into peace; they find rest as they lie in death.* ***3*** *"But you--come here, you sons of a sorceress, you* ***offspring of adulterers and prostitutes!*** ***4*** *Whom are you mocking? At whom do you sneer and stick out your tongue? Are you not a brood of rebels, the offspring of liars?* ***5*** *You* ***burn with lust among the oaks and under every spreading tree;*** *you sacrifice your children in the ravines and under the overhanging crags.* ***6*** *[The idols] among the smooth stones of the ravines are your portion; they, they are your lot. Yes, to them you have poured out drink offerings and offered grain offerings. In the light of these things, should I relent?* ***7 You have made your bed on a high and lofty hill****; there you went up to offer your sacrifices.* ***8*** *Behind your doors and your doorposts you have put your pagan symbols.* ***Forsaking me, you uncovered your bed, you climbed into it and opened it wide; you made a pact with those whose beds you love, and you looked on their nakedness.*** *9* ***You went to Molech with olive oil and increased your perfumes.*** *You sent your ambassadors far away; you descended to the grave itself !* ***10*** *You were wearied by all your ways, but you would not say, 'It is hopeless.' You found renewal of your strength, and so you did not faint.*

Judges 8:27

27 *Gideon made the gold into an* ***ephod****, which he placed in Ophrah, his town.* ***All Israel prostituted themselves by worshiping it there,*** *and it became a snare to Gideon and his family.*

Malachi 2:10-11
10 *Have we not all one Father? Did not one God create us? Why do we profane the covenant of our fathers by* ***breaking faith*** *with one another?* ***11*** *Judah has broken faith. A detestable thing has been committed in Israel and in Jerusalem: Judah has desecrated the sanctuary the LORD loves,* ***by marrying the daughter of a foreign god.***

Hosea 1:2
2 *When the LORD began to speak through Hosea, the LORD said to him, "Go, take to yourself an adulterous wife and children of unfaithfulness,* ***because the land is guilty of the vilest adultery in departing from the LORD."***

Hosea 2:2-5
2 *"Rebuke your mother, rebuke her, for she is not my wife, and I am not her husband. Let her remove* ***the adulterous look from her face*** *and the* ***unfaithfulness*** *from between her breasts.* ***3***
Otherwise I will strip her naked and make her as bare as on the day she was born; I will make her like a desert, turn her into a parched land, and slay her with thirst. ***4*** *I will not show my love to her children, because they are the children of* ***adultery****.*
5 Their mother has been unfaithful *and has conceived them in disgrace.* ***She said, 'I will go after my lovers****, who give me my food and my water, my wool and my linen, my oil and my drink.*

Hosea 5:3-4
3 *I know all about Ephraim; Israel is not hidden from me.* ***Ephraim, you have now turned to prostitution; Israel is corrupt.*** ***4*** *"Their deeds do not permit them to return to their God.* ***A spirit of prostitution is in their heart****; they do not acknowledge the LORD.*

Ezekiel 6:8-9
8 *" 'But I will spare some, for some of you will escape the sword when you are scattered among the lands and nations.* ***9*** *Then in the nations where they have been carried captive, those who escape will remember me--how I have been grieved by* ***their adulterous hearts****, which have turned away from me, and by their eyes, which have* ***lusted after their idols****. They will loathe themselves for the evil they have done and for all their detestable practices.*

See also *Ezekiel* chapters16 and 23 for graphic descriptions.

The concept of applying the term *adulterous* in the New Testament shows up in *Revelation 18:1-2; 14:8; 19:2; 17:1-5, 15-16* to describe how nations, kings and merchants commit adultery with Babylon the Great. Christians are called adulterers for being friends with the world *(James 4:1-6)*. The Pharisees and that generation which sought after signs were called adulterous *(Matthew 12:39; 16:4; Mark 8:38)*.

OTHER RELATIONSHIPS WITH IDOLS OR GODS INCLUDE LOOKING TO THEM FOR GUIDANCE, FEARING THEM, AND TRUSTING IN THEM.

Habakkuk 2:19
19 *Woe to him who says to wood, 'Come to life!' Or to lifeless stone, 'Wake up!'* ***Can it give guidance?*** *It is covered with gold and silver; there is no breath in it.*

Jeremiah 10:5
5 *Like a scarecrow in a melon patch, their idols cannot speak; they must be carried because they cannot walk.* ***Do not fear them****; they can do no harm nor can they do any good."*

Habakkuk 2:18
18 *"Of what value is an idol, since a man has carved it? Or an image that teaches lies? For he who makes it* ***trusts in his own creation****; he makes idols that cannot speak.*

Isaiah 42:17
17 *But those who* ***trust in idols****, who say to images, 'You are our gods,' will be turned back in utter shame.*

Jeremiah 13:25
25 *This is your lot, the portion I have decreed for you," declares the LORD, "because you have forgotten me and* ***trusted in false gods.***

GREED

Before we look at greed, we need to discuss a translation puzzle. This book uses the New International (NIV) translation of the Bible. In the NIV *Colossians 3:5* is translated using the English word **greed.**

> *Colossians 3:5 Put to death, therefore, whatever belongs to your earthly nature: sexual immorality, impurity, lust, evil desires and* ***greed****, which is idolatry.*

The New American Standard Version also uses the word **greed.** Some other translations (King James Version and English Standard Version) use the English word **covetousness** instead of greed. The Revised Standard Version uses the word **covetousness** but then the New Revised Standard Version uses the word **greed**. The differences in translation are not due to differences in Greek manuscripts.

The English words greed and covetousness are synonyms. They are similar, but also different.

Covetousness emphasizes the desire to have something that belongs to someone else. For example, the Law in *Exodus 20:17* states,

> *"You shall not **covet** your neighbor's house. You shall not **covet** your neighbor's wife, or his manservant or maidservant, his ox or donkey, or anything that **belongs to** your neighbor."*

This is of course the English translation of the Old Testament.

When the New Testament was translated into English, the translators uniformly used the English words for covet and covetousness in *Romans 7:7-8* which refers to the Law in *Exodus 20:17*. In other words, they translated the Greek using the English word covet (instead of be greedy for) because Paul is quoting the Law which emphasized desire for what "belongs to your neighbor" in the Law. Then, wherever those Greek words showed up elsewhere in the New Testament they consistently translated them like covetous and covetousness.

> *Romans 7:7-8*
> *"7 What shall we say, then? Is the law sin? Certainly not! Indeed I would not have known what sin was except through the law. For I would not have known what coveting really was if the law had not said, "**Do not covet**." 8 But sin, seizing the opportunity afforded by the commandment, produced in me every kind of **covetous desire**. For apart from law, sin is dead.)*

In contrast to covetousness, greed emphasizes the excessive desire for more, mainly in respect to money or possessions. For example, Jesus told his disciples to *be on their guard against all kinds of greed; a man's life does not consist in the abundance of his possessions (Luke 12:15)*. The issue came up because someone asked Jesus to make his brother give him his share of the inheritance. The man wanted what was his, not what belonged to his brother.

Luke 12:13-15
13 Someone in the crowd said to him, "Teacher, tell my brother to divide the inheritance with me." 14 Jesus replied, "Man, who appointed me a judge or an arbiter between you?" 15 Then he said to them, "Watch out! Be on your guard against all kinds of greed; a man's life does not consist in the abundance of his possessions."

We will also see that greed (or covetousness in some translations) is called idolatry. And that Jesus says we cannot love God and Mammon (money). So, the word greed (excessive desire for more) fits better with idolatry than the word covetousness (a desire to have what belongs to someone else.)

In both cases, greed (I want a lot of money or possessions) and covetousness (I want what you have) are sin for they oppose the two great commandments *(Matthew 22:34-40)*. To want a lot money or possessions is to not love God (the first great commandment). To want what belongs to someone else is to not love that person (the second great commandment). Both greed and covetousness are desire, but with different objects of the desire. The overlap would be if I desire money or possessions that belong to someone else.

In this book we will focus on greed.

Greed is not unique to the New Testament. God spoke of greed in the Old Testament, for example,

Jeremiah 6:13
From the least to the greatest, all are ***greedy*** *for gain; prophets and priests alike; all practice deceit.*

Proverbs 15:27
*A **greedy** man brings trouble to his family, but he who hates bribes will live.*

Proverbs 28:25
*A **greedy** man stirs up dissension, but he who trusts in the LORD will prosper.*

Proverbs 29:4
*By justice a king gives a country stability, but one who is **greedy** for bribes tears it down.*

However, under the Old Covenant, greed is not called idolatry. What is new to the New Testament is that under the New Covenant greed is called idolatry.

In this chapter we will look the concept of greed, why greed is called idolatry in the New Testament, and in particular how God determines what greed is. The latter is important because people today define greed much differently than God. People do this in order to avoid the term being applied to themselves – "others are greedy, but I am not."

A word search in the New Testament reveals the word greed or greedy is found as follows in the English Bible (NIV translation).

Matthew 23:25
*"Woe to you, teachers of the law and Pharisees, you hypocrites! You clean the outside of the cup and dish, but inside they are full of **greed** and self-indulgence.*

Mark 7:20-23
***20** He went on: "What comes out of a man is what makes him*
*'unclean.' **21** For from within, out of men's hearts, come evil*
*thoughts, sexual immorality, theft, murder, adultery, **22 greed**,*

malice, deceit, lewdness, envy, slander, arrogance and folly. **23**
All these evils come from inside and make a man 'unclean.' "

Luke 11:39
Then the Lord said to him, "Now then, you Pharisees clean the outside of the cup and dish, but inside you are full of ***greed*** *and wickedness.*

Luke 12:15
Then he said to them, "Watch out! Be on your guard against all kinds of ***greed****; a man's life does not consist in the abundance of his possessions."*

Romans 1:29
They have become filled with every kind of wickedness, evil, ***greed*** *and depravity. They are full of envy, murder, strife, deceit and malice. They are gossips,*

1 Corinthians 5:10-11
...not at all meaning the people of this world who are immoral, or the ***greedy*** *and swindlers, or idolaters. In that case you would have to leave this world. But now I am writing you that you must not associate with anyone who calls himself a brother but is sexually immoral or* ***greedy****, an idolater or a slanderer, a drunkard or a swindler. With such a man do not even eat.*

1 Corinthians 6:10
...nor thieves nor the ***greedy*** *nor drunkards nor slanderers nor swindlers will inherit the kingdom of God.*

Ephesians 5:3
But among you there must not be even a hint of sexual immorality, or of any kind of impurity, or of ***greed****, because these are improper for God's holy people.*

Ephesians 5:5
For of this you can be sure: No immoral, impure or ***greedy*** *person--such a man is an idolater--has any inheritance in the kingdom of Christ and of God.*

Colossians 3:5
Put to death, therefore, whatever belongs to your earthly nature: sexual immorality, impurity, lust, evil desires and ***greed****, which is idolatry.*

1 Thessalonians 2:5
You know we never used flattery, nor did we put on a mask to cover up ***greed****--God is our witness.*

1 Peter 5:2
Be shepherds of God's flock that is under your care, serving as overseers--not because you must, but because you are willing, as God wants you to be; not ***greedy*** *for money, but eager to serve;*

2 Peter 2:3
In their ***greed*** *these teachers will exploit you with stories they have made up. Their condemnation has long been hanging over them, and their destruction has not been sleeping.*

2 Peter 2:14
With eyes full of adultery, they never stop sinning; they seduce the unstable; they are experts in ***greed****--an accursed brood!*

First of all, greed is the normal state for those who have willfully rejected God (*1 Corinthians 5:10*). *Romans 1:18-31* describes steps or stages of a society. They willfully suppress the truth *(v19-20)* about God by their wickedness. They enter into physical idolatry *(v 23, 25)*. Therefore God turns them over (gives them over to another power) to sexual impurity *(v 24)* including lesbianism and homosexuality *(v26-27)* and a depraved mind *(v28)*. They become filled with many evils *(v 29-32)*, only one of which is greed *(v29)*. Gossip is also one of the evils. We should not be surprised by this. We should also not be judgmental about this, for each of us were also under the dominion of darkness when God rescued us and brought us into the kingdom of the Son (*Colossians 1:13; 1 Corinthians 6:10)*. Like the rest, we were also objects of God's wrath (*Ephesians 2:1-3)*. So, let's not be judgmental of the normal state of people, including their greed.

> *Romans 1:18-31*
> ***18** The wrath of God is being revealed from heaven against all the godlessness and wickedness of men who suppress the truth by their wickedness, **19** since what may be known about God is plain to them, because God has made it plain to them. **20** For since the creation of the world God's invisible qualities--his eternal power and divine nature--have been clearly seen, being understood from what has been made, so that men are without excuse. **21** For although they knew God, they neither glorified him as God nor gave thanks to him, but their thinking became futile and their foolish hearts were darkened. **22** Although they claimed to be wise, they became fools **23** and exchanged the glory of the immortal God for images made to look like mortal man and birds and animals and reptiles. **24** Therefore God gave them over in the sinful desires of their hearts to sexual impurity for the degrading of their bodies with one another. **25** They exchanged the truth of God for a lie, and worshiped and served created things rather than the Creator--who is forever praised. Amen. **26** Because of this, God gave them over to shameful lusts. Even their women exchanged natural relations for unnatural ones. **27** In the same*

way the men also abandoned natural relations with women and were inflamed with lust for one another. Men committed indecent acts with other men, and received in themselves the due penalty for their perversion. ***28*** *Furthermore, since they did not think it worthwhile to retain the knowledge of God, he gave them over to a depraved mind, to do what ought not to be done.* ***29*** *They have become filled with every kind of wickedness, evil,* ***greed*** *and depravity. They are full of envy, murder, strife, deceit and malice. They are gossips,* ***30*** *slanderers, God-haters, insolent, arrogant and boastful; they invent ways of doing evil; they disobey their parents;* ***31*** *they are senseless, faithless, heartless, ruthless.* ***32*** *Although they know God's righteous decree that those who do such things deserve death, they not only continue to do these very things but also approve of those who practice them.*

There were those who were full of greed, but hid their greed. These were the teachers of the law and Pharisees. (*Matthew 23:25; Luke 11:39; 12:15*).

False teachers appear to be driven by greed (*2 Peter 2:3, 14*).

Overseers of God's flock are to not be greedy for money (*1 Peter 5:2*).

Christians should not be greedy (*Ephesians 5:3; Colossians 3:5*).

Greed is inconsistent with inheriting the kingdom of God (*1 Corinthians 6:10; Ephesians 5:5*).

Believers are not to associate or eat with anyone who calls himself a brother but is sexually immoral or greedy, an idolater or a slanderer, a drunkard or a swindler. (*1 Corinthians 5:11)*

So, we can understand why Christians in particular do not want to identify themselves with greed --- just as the Israelites did not want to identify themselves with idolatry. Under the Old Covenant if you knew of another Israelite who was involved with idolatry and encouraged others to be also, the command was not whether you could associate or eat with the person – they were to be put to death! (*Deuteronomy 13)*

Now there are two Scriptures that differentiate between greed and idolatry, and two Scripture that say greed is idolatry. *1 Corinthians 5:10* and *5:11* mention greedy as separate from idolater. On the other hand, *Ephesians 5:5* says a greedy person is an idolater, and *Colossians 3:5* says that greed is idolatry. The difference may be that in the Corinthian church there was considerable discussion about eating food offered to physical idols and fleeing physical idolatry (*1 Corinthians 8* and *10*), so that the *1 Corinthian 5:10* and *5:11* idolaters were involved with physical idols.

1 Corinthians 5:10-11
...not at all meaning the people of this world who are immoral, or the ***greedy*** *and swindlers,* ***or idolaters****. In that case you would have to leave this world. But now I am writing you that you must not associate with anyone who calls himself a brother but is sexually immoral or* ***greedy****,* ***an idolater*** *or a slanderer, a drunkard or a swindler. With such a man do not even eat.*

Ephesians 5:5
For of this you can be sure: No immoral, impure or ***greedy*** *person--such a man is an idolater--has any inheritance in the kingdom of Christ and of God.*

Colossians 3:5
Put to death, therefore, whatever belongs to your earthly nature: sexual immorality, impurity, lust, evil desires and ***greed****, which is idolatry.*

What is greed? Webster defines it as excessive desire for acquiring or having; desire for more than one needs or deserves. (Note that greed is a desire, so the measure of greed is the strength of the desire, not how much one has. So, someone with little can be in principle more greedy than someone with a lot.) This concept of excessive desire for acquiring or having more than one needs or deserves is consistent with *1 Peter 5:2* "*greedy for money*" and *Luke 12:5* "*greedy for possessions.*"

However, the *Luke 12:15* passage is more challenging in context. Let's look at this more closely. A man wants Jesus to tell his brother to divide the inheritance with him *(v 13)*. There is no indication that this claim is bogus, i.e., the inheritance should be divided. But Jesus basically says the man who wanted the inheritance divided was greedy *(v 15)*! Now think of yourself. Let's say your parents die and leave you and your brother an inheritance, but your brother is the only one with access to the cash, stocks, bonds or the deed of property. You and your brother know what the will says, but he will not give you what your parents says is yours. How would you react if your spiritual leader called you greedy when this was owed to you, what you have a right to? Now that is the dilemma in this passage.

But things get even more precarious as we continue with the passage. Jesus first tells a parable to the hearers *(v 16-21)*. The parable addresses a rich man who was able to build a large retirement program. In the parable Jesus is hard on the rich man for storing up for himself instead of being rich toward God. Now that message is only troubling for the rich; those without the ability to build a large retirement program of course say to themselves,

"Go get him, Jesus!" Next Jesus gives direct teaching *(v 22-34)* to his disciples, none of whom are rich, to not worry about food and clothing for God will provide those; instead they are to sell their possessions and give to the poor *(v 33)*, the poor being those without food or clothing.

Now, the hearer may get very nervous, and the dilemma is revealed. Yes, the man who had not received his inheritance had a right to it, but he was greedy to demand it, for this showed that the man **believed** his life consisted in the abundance of his possessions – **the evidence of greed**. This leads us to a discussion of how God determines if there is greed, or rather how God determines if there is **excessive** desire for acquiring or having; desire for **more than one needs or deserves.** If from God's perspective all that one needs is food and clothing, then greed is to want more than food and clothing. That hits almost all of us, **including those below the "poverty level"** of about $23,000 for a family of four, as defined by the U.S. government in 2013.

> *Luke 12:13-34*
> ***13*** *Someone in the crowd said to him, "Teacher,*
> *tell my brother to divide the inheritance with me."*
> ***14*** *Jesus replied, "Man, who appointed me a judge*
> *or an arbiter between you?"* ***15*** *Then he said to*
> *them,* ***"Watch out! Be on your guard against all***
> ***kinds of greed; a man's life does not consist in***
> ***the abundance of his possessions****."* ***16*** *And he*
> *told them this parable: "The ground of a certain*
> *rich man produced a good crop.* ***17*** *He thought*
> *to himself, 'What shall I do? I have no place to*
> *store my crops.'* ***18*** *"Then he said, 'This is what*
> *I'll do. I will tear down my barns and build bigger*
> *ones, and there I will store all my grain and my*
> *goods.* ***19*** *And I'll say to myself, "You have plenty*
> *of good things laid up for many years. Take life*

easy; eat, drink and be merry." ' **20** *"But God*
said to him, 'You fool! This very night your life
will be demanded from you. Then who will get
what you have prepared for yourself?' **21** *"This*
is how it will be with anyone who stores up things
for himself but is not rich toward God." **22** *Then*
Jesus said to his disciples: "Therefore I tell you,
do not worry about your life, what you will eat;
or about your body, what you will wear. **23** *Life is*
more than food, and the body more than clothes.
24 *Consider the ravens: They do not sow or reap,*
they have no storeroom or barn; yet God feeds
them. And how much more valuable you are than
birds! **25** *Who of you by worrying can add a single*
hour to his life? **26** *Since you cannot do this very*
little thing, why do you worry about the rest? **27**
"Consider how the lilies grow. They do not labor
or spin. Yet I tell you, not even Solomon in all his
splendor was dressed like one of these. **28** *If that*
is how God clothes the grass of the field, which
is here today, and tomorrow is thrown into the
fire, how much more will he clothe you, O you of
little faith! **29** *And do not set your heart on what*
you will eat or drink; do not worry about it. **30**
For the pagan world runs after all such things,
and your Father knows that you need them. **31**
But seek his kingdom, and these things will be
given to you as well. **32** *"Do not be afraid, little*
flock, for your Father has been pleased to give
you the kingdom. **33** *Sell your possessions and*
give to the poor. Provide purses for yourselves
that will not wear out, a treasure in heaven that
will not be exhausted, where no thief comes near
and no moth destroys. **34** *For where your treasure*
is, there your heart will be also.

So, the above teaching of Jesus sets a baseline for greed as desiring more than food and clothing.

A similar teaching of Jesus shows up in the Sermon of the Mount *(Matthew 6:24-34)*. In this case the word greed or greedy does not show up, but the concept of serving either God or Money does come up. (This gives a hint about the tie between greed and idolatry.)

Another way to see the baseline for greed is to look at the opposite of greed – contentment. The baseline for contentment is also food and clothing

1 Timothy 6:6 reveals that godliness with contentment is great gain.

1 Timothy 6:6-7
6 *But godliness with contentment is great gain.* ***7*** *For we brought*
nothing into the world, and we can take nothing out of it.

How much then is enough to be content? *I Timothy 6:8* reveals that food and clothing are enough to be content. Uh oh!

1 Timothy 6:8
8 *But if we have food and clothing, we will be content with that.*

Proverbs 30:7-9 reveals that daily bread is enough because without it one will steal and dishonor the name of God. But having "too much" may lead a person to disown God and say, "Who is the Lord? *(i.e., I don't need God anymore.)*

Proverbs 30:7-9
7 *"Two things I ask of you, O LORD; do not refuse me before I*
die: ***8*** *Keep falsehood and lies far from me; give me neither pov-*
erty nor riches, but give me only my daily bread. ***9*** *Otherwise, I*

may have too much and disown you and say, 'Who is the LORD?' Or I may become poor and steal, and so dishonor the name of my God.

What happens if we want more than being content with food and clothing? *I Timothy 6:9-10* shows the slippery slope.

1 Timothy 6:9-10
9 People who want to get rich fall into temptation and a trap and into many foolish and harmful desires that plunge men into ruin and destruction. 10 For the love of money is a root of all kinds of evil. Some people, eager for money, have wandered from the faith and pierced themselves with many griefs.

The slippery slope, as revealed in *1 Timothy 6:9-10,* looks like this:

We fall into temptation first (tempted to get more than food and clothing by using injustice according to God's standard.)

Then we enter a trap – we grasp for "much gain." We ignore any injustice by denying it exists (for example, "I am not violating God's standard!" Or, "God's standard is old fashioned!" Or, "I could care less about God's standard!" etc.)

What follows next is that foolish and harmful desires are generated as a result of being in the trap.

Then these desires lead to ruin and destruction because these desires influence wrong decisions. *Ecclesiastes 5:10* indicates that the desire for money (love of money) cannot be satisfied; the foolish and harmful desires cannot be satisfied – they grow. Note in *Ecclesiastes* 5:10 that whoever loves wealth is never satisfied with his income. Are you satisfied with your income? What does that reveal about you?

Ecclesiastes 5:10
Whoever loves money never has money enough; whoever loves wealth is never satisfied with his income. This too is meaningless.

This slippery slope can even lead people of faith to wander from their faith and pierce themselves with many griefs.

Note also that the demarcation between poverty and riches is having daily bread in *Proverbs 30:7-9*.

Proverbs 30:7-9
7 "Two things I ask of you, O LORD; do not refuse me before I
die: ***8*** *Keep falsehood and lies far from me;* ***give me neither poverty nor riches, but give me only my daily bread. 9*** *Otherwise, I*
may have too much and disown you and say, 'Who is the LORD?' Or I may become poor and steal, and so dishonor the name of my God.

Now the baseline for greed is obviously much different than our perspective today. In fact, the term poverty level in the Western world is actually "rich" from God's viewpoint. Furthermore, much of the third world today would find the Western poverty level as rich for them even on human terms. That there are great differences among the "rich" in the Western world is very true, but Western politics are about reducing the range between the very rich and the less rich. The "less rich" (from God's perspective) are greedy to become more rich -- out of envy, or in some cases maybe covetousness.

But our interest in this book is not about politics but about God's people and greed.

There is one aspect to idolatry that needs to be made clear -- that shows this subject is not some academic exercise in Biblical study or knowledge. This is very serious. God is not in the business of enabling, nor being co-dependent, nor looking the other way. We must not mistake the fact that He is long-suffering for His approval. He is jealous for His people's sake, both under the Old Covenant and the New Covenant. We will see later how His jealously took action under the Old Covenant. He is no less jealous of the Church, the Bride of His Son, than He was of Israel, His Wife.

Colossians 3:5-6
5 *Put to death, therefore, whatever belongs to your earthly nature: sexual immorality, impurity, lust, evil desires and* ***greed, which is idolatry. 6 Because of these, the wrath of God is coming.***

Ephesians 5:3-6
3 *But among you there must not be even a hint of sexual immorality, or of any kind of impurity, or of* ***greed,*** *because these are improper for God's holy people.* ***4*** *Nor should there be obscenity, foolish talk or coarse joking, which are out of place, but rather thanksgiving.* ***5*** *For of this you can be sure: No immoral, impure or* ***greedy person--such a man is an idolater****--has any inheritance in the kingdom of Christ and of God.* ***6*** *Let no one deceive you with empty words, for* ***because of such things God's wrath comes on those who are disobedient.***

DEBT AND GREED

The overall consumer debt in the U.S. peaked in the 3rd quarter of 2008 at $12.7 trillion dollars (re. Federal Reserve Bank of New York, "Quarterly Report on Household Debt and Credit," November 2012.) Of this about $8.8 trillion was in mortgage debt with the remaining spread across student loans, auto loans, credit cards, home-equity loans, and other. The overall consumer debt in the U.S. dropped to $11.3 trillion in the 3rd quarter of 2012. This is consumer debt, not corporate and government debt. In 2010 about 75% of American families had outstanding debt, and 25% did not.

In contrast, the 3rd quarter 2012 overall personal income in the U.S. was $13.4 trillion (http://www.bea.gov/scb/pdf/2013/02%20 February/0213_gdpecon.pdf.) So, in the 3rd quarter of 2012 the U.S. consumer income was $1.19 for every $1.00 in debt ($13.4 trillion divided by $11.2 trillion). This is part of the American dream to have prosperity today based upon expectations for tomorrow.

The question for this chapter -- "Is personal debt a symptom of greed?"

The Old Covenant allowed debt, and provided some regulations on debt, for example as in *Deuteronomy 15:1-11*. Of particular interest is that at the end of 7 years, all debts were to be cancelled even if they had not been paid. In addition, the loans were to be given to the poor and needy fellow Israelites.

Deuteronomy 15:1-11
1 At the end of every seven years you must cancel debts. ***2*** *This is how it is to be done: Every creditor shall cancel the loan he has made to his fellow Israelite.* ***He shall not require payment from his fellow Israelite or brother****, because the LORD's time for canceling debts has been proclaimed.* ***3*** *You may require payment from a foreigner, but you must cancel any debt your brother owes you.* ***4*** *However, there should be no poor among you, for in the land the LORD your God is giving you to possess as your inheritance, he will richly bless you,* ***5*** *if only you fully obey the LORD your God and are careful to follow all these commands I am giving you today.* ***6*** *For the LORD your God will bless you as he has promised, and you will lend to many nations but will borrow from none. You will rule over many nations but none will rule over you.* ***7*** *If there is a* ***poor man among your brothers*** *in any of the towns of the land that the LORD your God is giving you, do not be hardhearted or tightfisted toward your poor brother.* ***8*** *Rather be openhanded and freely lend him whatever he needs.* ***9*** *Be careful not to harbor this wicked thought: "The seventh year, the year for canceling debts, is near," so that you do not show ill will toward* ***your needy brother*** *and give him nothing. He may then appeal to the LORD against you, and you will be found guilty of sin.* ***10*** *Give generously to him and do so without a grudging heart; then because of this the LORD your God*

> *will bless you in all your work and in everything you put your hand to.* ***11*** *There will always be poor people in the land. Therefore I command you to be* ***openhanded toward your brothers and toward the poor and needy*** *in your land.*

Under the New Covenant, however, we find that we are to let no debt remain outstanding, except the debt to love one another (*Romans 13:18-10*).

> *Romans 13:8-10*
> ***8 Let no debt remain outstanding, except the continuing debt to love one another****, for he who loves his fellowman has fulfilled the law.* ***9*** *The commandments, "Do not commit adultery," "Do not murder," "Do not steal," "Do not covet," and whatever other commandment there may be, are summed up in this one rule: "Love your neighbor as yourself."* ***10*** *Love does no harm to its neighbor. Therefore love is the fulfillment of the law.*

So, the question is, "What does it mean to let no debt remain outstanding?" Does that mean pay your debts on time, or does it mean you should have no debts at all? Christians have been divided over the interpretation.

If it means pay your debts on time, then this implies you, or God, will control your future so that you always have the money to pay your debts on time. Right? Note it does not say "Let no debt remain outstanding as long as you have the money to pay the debt on time."

James 4:13-16 addresses a similar issue. It shows that we do not know what will happen tomorrow, and to claim we do is boasting and all such boasting is evil. So, we do not have the ability to be sure we will have the money tomorrow to pay for the debt that is due to tomorrow.

> *James 4:13-16*
> ***13** Now listen, you who say, "**Today or tomorrow we will go to this or that city, spend a year there, carry on business and make money**." **14** Why, **you do not even know what will happen tomorrow**. What is your life? You are a mist that appears for a little while and then vanishes. **15** Instead, you ought to say, "**If it is the Lord's will**, we will live and do this or that." **16** As it is, you boast and brag. **All such boasting is evil.***

So, can we count on God to make sure we have the money tomorrow to pay tomorrow's debt? The *James 4:13-16* passage indicates we do not know for sure if God will do that for us. It says, "If it is the Lord's will..." And we do not know if it is the Lord's will.

What God does promise us for tomorrow is food and clothing if we seek first his kingdom (*Matthew 6:25-34*). He does not promise to give us more than food and clothing if we seek first his kingdom. We are to be content with food and clothing *(1 Timothy 6:8)*.

> *Matthew 6:25-34*
> ***25 "Therefore I tell you, do not worry about your life, what you will eat or drink; or about your body, what you will wear**. Is not life more important than food, and the body more important than clothes? **26** Look at the birds of the air; they do not sow or reap or store away in barns, and yet your heavenly Father feeds them. Are you not*

> *much more valuable than they?* ***27*** *Who of you by worrying can add a single hour to his life?* ***28*** *"And why do you worry about clothes? See how the lilies of the field grow. They do not labor or spin.* ***29*** *Yet I tell you that not even Solomon in all his splendor was dressed like one of these.* ***30*** *If that is how God clothes the grass of the field, which is here today and tomorrow is thrown into the fire, will he not much more clothe you, O you of little faith?* ***31 So do not worry, saying, 'What shall we eat?' or 'What shall we drink?' or 'What shall we wear?' 32*** *For the pagans run after all these things, and your heavenly Father knows that you need them.* ***33 But seek first his kingdom and his righteousness, and all these things will be given to you as well. 34*** *Therefore do not worry about tomorrow, for tomorrow will worry about itself. Each day has enough trouble of its own.*

What exactly is debt? It is the borrowing of money so we can possess something today instead of tomorrow when we have saved up the money. That smells like greed.

Or, it is the borrowing of money in order to invest in something that we hope to gain tomorrow, such as more money or a job or recovered health. The gain of more money smells like greed, but do the others? That is not so clear.

I thought I would close this discussion with a sermon I heard in the 1980's. The question was about mortgage debt and the *Romans 13* passage. The pastor argued that if one looked at the history of housing debt crises in the U.S., you would find that the worst drop in housing prices was 25% since the Great

Depression. So, he argued that a Christian should have a minimum of 25% down payment when buying a house. Sounded reasonable.

Of course that criteria was blown out of the water by the recent Great Recession (2008)! And huge numbers of people worldwide, including Christians, did not pay their debts on time -- or ever. Government stepped in to avoid economic collapse, rebellion, and anarchy. Then they assigned blame to everyone but the consumers (voters) who took out the debt. Then, political parties proposed competing plans to return the consumer (voters) to the American Dream.

The reality is none of us know what tomorrow brings.

> *Ecclesiastes 8*
> *7 Since no man knows the future, who can tell him what is to come?*
>
> *Ecclesiastes 9*
> *11 I have seen something else under the sun: The race is not to the swift or the battle to the strong, nor does food come to the wise or wealth to the brilliant or favor to the learned; but time and chance happen to them all. 12 Moreover, no man knows when his hour will come: As fish are caught in a cruel net, or birds are taken in a snare, so men are trapped by evil times that fall unexpectedly upon them.*

Why is greed called idolatry under the New Covenant?

Greed (which is a desire) and idolatry (with man-made physical idols) seem very different from each other, so why under the New Covenant does greed become idolatry?

To answer that we first need a short description of the Old versus New Covenants.

The Old Covenant was an agreement called a "covenant" between God and his people the Israelites (*Exodus 19:5-6; 34:10-11, 28)* where the covenant was written on tablets of stone (*Exodus 24:12; 34:1)* by God and given to Moses. The covenant was based upon the Ten Commandments (*Exodus 20:1-17; 34:28)* but extended to all the words and laws God gave Moses (*Exodus 24:3-4)*. Part of the Covenant was to not make, or bow down to, or worship idols. The Book of the Law was placed beside the ark of the covenant which the tribe of the Levites carried; this was done as **a witness against the Israelites** (*Deuteronomy 31:26)* for they were a rebellious and stiff-necked people. In other words from the early days of the Old Covenant it was clear the Israelites would not keep the covenant.

Hundreds of years later, in the days of the prophet Jeremiah, Judah (two southern tribes of Israel) would be carried into captivity by Babylon because of their idolatry. Before they were taken away by Babylon, God told Jeremiah that he would make a New Covenant (thus the previous covenant is called the Old Covenant) with his people.

> *Jeremiah 31:31-34*
> ***31*** *"The time is coming," declares the LORD, "when I will make a* ***new covenant*** *with the house of Israel and with the house of Judah.* ***32*** *It will not be like the covenant I made with their forefathers when I took them by the hand to lead them out of Egypt, because they broke my covenant, though I was a husband to them, " declares the LORD.* ***33*** *"This is the covenant I will make with the house of Israel after that time," declares the LORD.* ***"I will put my law in their minds and write it on their hearts****. I will be their God, and they will be my people.* ***34*** *No longer will a man teach his neighbor, or a man his brother, saying, 'Know the LORD,' because they will all know me, from the least of them to the greatest," declares the LORD. "For I will forgive their wickedness and will remember their sins no more."*

In the New Covenant the law would be put in the minds and written on the hearts, instead of on stone as under the Old Covenant. When we come to the New Testament (*Hebrews 8:6-13)* we find this same New Covenant as related to Jesus *(v 6)*. There was something wrong *(v 7)* with the Old Covenant that brought the need for the New Covenant. The fault in the Old Covenant was with the people *(v 8)*. Also, the New Covenant made the Old Covenant obsolete *(v 13)*.

Hebrews 8:6-13
***6** But the ministry Jesus has received is as superior to theirs as the covenant of which he is mediator is superior to the old one, and it is founded on better promises. **7** For if there had been nothing wrong with that first covenant, no place would have been sought for another. **8** But God found fault with the people and said: "The time is coming, declares the Lord, when I will make a new covenant with the house of Israel and with the house of Judah. **9** It will not be like the covenant I made with their forefathers when I took them by the hand to lead them out of Egypt, because they did not remain faithful to my covenant, and I turned away from them, declares the Lord. **10** This is the covenant I will make with the house of Israel after that time, declares the Lord. I will put my laws in their minds and write them on their hearts. I will be their God, and they will be my people. **11** No longer will a man teach his neighbor, or a man his brother, saying, 'Know the Lord,' because they will all know me, from the least of them to the greatest. **12** For I will forgive their wickedness and will remember their sins no more." **13** By calling this covenant "new," he has made the first one obsolete; and what is obsolete and aging will soon disappear.*

One more key point is that the reference to the New Covenant is repeated in *Hebrews 10:15-17*, but in this case we find the Holy Spirit is the One who puts the laws in their hearts and writes them on their minds.

Hebrews 10:12-17
***12** But when this priest [Jesus Christ} had offered for all time one sacrifice for sins, he sat down*

> *at the right hand of God.* ***13*** *Since that time he waits for his enemies to be made his footstool,* ***14*** *because by one sacrifice he has made perfect forever those who are being made holy.* ***15 The Holy Spirit also testifies to us about this. First he says: 16*** *"This is the covenant I will make with them after that time, says the Lord.* ***I will put my laws in their hearts, and I will write them on their minds****."* ***17*** *Then he adds: "Their sins and lawless acts I will remember no more."*

To summarize, the New Covenant is related to Jesus and has the Holy Spirit do the writing of the law on hearts and minds of God's people. If you think about it, this makes sense that the Holy Spirit would do the writing since it is on our hearts and in our minds and the Holy Spirit indwells God's people.

Now let's look at the Sermon on the Mount to see how the "law" changes from the Old Covenant to the New Covenant. The law changes in the sense that it broadens out to the heart. Murder broadens out to anger with one's brother, and adultery broadens out to looking at a woman lustfully. Murder and adultery are done in the flesh (under the Old Covenant law was written on stone), and anger and lust are done in the heart as well (under the New Covenant law is written on the hearts).

> *Matthew 5:21-27*
> ***21*** *"You have heard that it was said to the people long ago,* ***'Do not murder, and anyone who murders will be subject to judgment.' 22 But I tell you that anyone who is angry with his brother will be subject to judgment****. Again, anyone who says to his brother, 'Raca,' is answerable to the Sanhedrin. But anyone who says, 'You fool!' will be in danger of the fire of hell.* ***23*** *"Therefore,*

> *if you are offering your gift at the altar and there remember that your brother has something against you,* ***24*** *leave your gift there in front of the altar. First go and be reconciled to your brother; then come and offer your gift.* ***25*** *"Settle matters quickly with your adversary who is taking you to court. Do it while you are still with him on the way, or he may hand you over to the judge, and the judge may hand you over to the officer, and you may be thrown into prison.* ***26*** *I tell you the truth, you will not get out until you have paid the last penny.*
>
> *27* ***"You have heard that it was said, 'Do not commit adultery.' 28 But I tell you that anyone who looks at a woman lustfully has already committed adultery with her in his heart.***

We could spend a great amount of time showing how physical-related things under the Old Covenant expand to spiritual-related things under the New Covenant (for example, the rest, the priesthood, the tabernacle under the Old Covenant -- and the work of Christ under the New Covenant, *Hebrews* chapters *4, 7-10)*. But the key is that just as anger is related to murder, and lust is related to adultery, so greed is related to idolatry. In each case one is related to the heart (anger, lust, greed) and the other to the physical (murder, adultery, idolatry). Under the New Covenant, what is in the heart is equivalent from God's perspective to what was physical under the Old Covenant. While the New Covenant broadens God's law to the heart, the Holy Spirit who is the writer of the law on the heart is also given so that by walking by the Spirit we need not fulfill the sinful desires of the heart.

How then are greed in the heart and idolatry in the physical related to each other? Greed is the desire in the heart to have more money or possessions for ourselves (beyond basic food and clothing) and reveals we are serving Money rather than God. Jesus said we could not serve both, so in greed we displace serving God in our heart with serving Money in our heart. (In physical idolatry we displace serving God with serving idols.)

Matthew 6
24 "No one can serve two masters. Either he will hate the one and love the other, or he will be devoted to the one and despise the other. You cannot ***serve*** *both God and* ***Money****.*

WHAT HAPPENS TO THOSE WHO HAVE IDOLS?

There were many, many things that happened to God's people when they had idols in the Old Testament. The list is very long and sad and sobering.

- They harm themselves.
- They defile the land, the city, and themselves.
- God gives them over to a stubborn heart to follow their own devices.
- They desecrate or defile the sanctuary the Lord loves.
- They became enslaved.
- They are led astray.
- They become cursed.
- They want to get away from the Lord.
- They become useless (and may feel useless).
- They forfeit God's favor.
- They become joined to idols; a union is formed.
- They become ignorant.
- They increase their sorrows.
- They may fear their gods (instead of fearing the Lord).
- They may boast in their idols.
- Their hearts turn away from the Lord and become devoted to idols.

- They look to their idols.
- They consecrate themselves to their idols and become as vile as the idol they love.
- Their prosperity leads to more idolatry.
- They stumble in their ways.
- They become detestable.
- They trust in their idols and are turned back in shame.
- They are defrauded.
- The silver and gold they use to make idols and images will not help them when God's wrath comes. The silver and gold only makes them stumble into sin.
- Their idolatry becomes tiring, but they find strength to pursue it anyway.
- They lack the wisdom to find the "opening of the womb" when the Lord brings deliverance from idolatry.
- They try to hide their idolatry from the Lord.
- They sell themselves to do evil.
- They embrace their gods.
- They become like their idols in that they cannot speak, see, hear, talk, smell, feel, or walk.
- They become defenseless to their enemies, because the Lord hands them over.
- They forgot God, and deserted Him for idols.
- Their spiritual blindness became enormous.

SUPPORTING VERSES ARE LISTED NEXT.

- They harm themselves.

Jeremiah 7:6
6 *if you do not oppress the alien, the fatherless or the widow and do not shed innocent blood in this place, and if you do not follow other gods to* ***your own harm****,*

Jeremiah 7:18-19
18** The children gather wood, the fathers light the fire, and the women knead the dough and make cakes of bread for the Queen of Heaven. They pour out drink offerings to other gods to provoke me to anger.* ***19** But am I the one they are provoking? declares the LORD. Are they not rather* ***harming themselves*, to their own shame?*

- They defile the land, the city, and themselves.

Ezekiel 36:17-18
17** "Son of man, when the people of Israel were living in their own land, they* ***defiled *it by their conduct and their actions. Their conduct was like a woman's monthly uncleanness in my sight.* ***18*** *So I poured out my wrath on them because they had shed blood in the land and because they had* ***defiled*** *it with their idols.*

Ezekiel 22:1-4
1** The word of the LORD came to me:* ***2** "Son of man, will you judge her? Will you judge this city [Jerusalem]of bloodshed? Then confront her with all her detestable practices* ***3** and say: 'This is what the Sovereign LORD says:* ***O city *that brings on herself doom by shedding blood in her midst and* ***defiles herself by making idols, 4*** *you have become guilty because of the blood you have shed and have become* ***defiled by the idols you have made****. You have brought your days to a close, and the end of your years has come. Therefore I will make you an object of scorn to the nations and a laughingstock to all the countries.*

Psalms 106:38-39
38** They shed innocent blood, the blood of their sons and daughters,* ***whom they sacrificed to the idols of Canaan*, and the land was desecrated by their blood.* ***39 They defiled themselves*** *by what they did; by their deeds they prostituted themselves.*

Ezekiel 20:18, 26, 31
18 *I said to their children in the desert, "Do not follow the statutes of your fathers or keep their laws or* ***defile yourselves*** *with their idols.*

26 *I let* ***them become defiled*** *through their gifts--the sacrifice of every firstborn--that I might fill them with horror so they would know that I am the LORD.'*

31 *When you offer your gifts--the sacrifice of your sons in the fire--you continue to* ***defile yourselves*** *with all your idols to this day. Am I to let you inquire of me, O house of Israel? As surely as I live, declares the Sovereign LORD, I will not let you inquire of me.*

Jeremiah 16:18
18 *I will repay them double for their wickedness and their sin, because they have defiled my land with the lifeless forms of their vile images and have filled my inheritance with their detestable idols."*

- God gives them over to a stubborn heart to follow their own devices.

Psalms 81:8-12
8 *"Hear, O my people, and I will warn you-- if you would but*
listen to me, O Israel! ***9*** *You shall have no foreign god among*
you; you shall not bow down to an alien god. ***10*** *I am the LORD*
your God, who brought you up out of Egypt. Open wide your
mouth and I will fill it. ***11*** *"But my people would not listen to me;*
Israel would not submit to me. ***12*** *So* ***I gave them over to their stubborn hearts to follow their own devices.***

- They desecrate or defile the sanctuary the Lord loves.

Malachi 2:11
***11** Judah has broken faith. A detestable thing has been committed in Israel and in Jerusalem: Judah has **desecrated the sanctuary the LORD loves**, by marrying the daughter of a foreign god.*

Ezekiel 23:39
***39** On the very day they sacrificed their children to their idols, they entered **my sanctuary and desecrated it**. That is what they did in my house.*

Ezekiel 5:11
***11** Therefore as surely as I live, declares the Sovereign LORD, because you have **defiled my sanctuary** with all your vile images and detestable practices, I myself will withdraw my favor; I will not look on you with pity or spare you.*

- They became enslaved.

Hosea 5:3-4
***3** I know all about Ephraim; Israel is not hidden from me. Ephraim, you have now turned to prostitution; Israel is corrupt.*
***4** "Their deeds do not permit them to return to their God**. A spirit of prostitution is in their heart; they do not acknowledge the LORD.*

Psalms 106:34-36
***34** They did not destroy the peoples as the LORD had commanded them, **35** but they mingled with the nations and adopted their customs. **36** They **worshiped their idols, which became a snare** to them.*

- They are led astray.

Hosea 4:12
12 *of my people. They consult a wooden idol and are answered by a stick of wood.* ***A spirit of prostitution leads them astray; they are unfaithful to their God.***

Amos 2:4
4 *This is what the LORD says: "For three sins of Judah, even for four, I will not turn back [my wrath]. Because they have rejected the law of the LORD and have not kept his decrees, because they have been* ***led astray by false gods****, the gods their ancestors followed,*

Jeremiah 23:13
13 *"Among the prophets of Samaria I saw this repulsive thing: They prophesied by Baal* ***and led my people Israel astray****.*

- They become cursed.

Deuteronomy 27:15
15 *"Cursed is the man who carves an image or casts an idol--a thing detestable to the LORD, the work of the craftsman's hands--and sets it up in secret." Then all the people shall say, "Amen!"*

- They want to get away from the Lord.

Hosea 11:2
2 *But the more I called Israel,* ***the further they went from me****. They sacrificed to the Baals and they burned incense to images.*

- They become useless (and may feel useless).

Jeremiah 13:10
***10** These wicked people, who refuse to listen to my words, who follow the stubbornness of their hearts and go after other gods to serve and worship them, **will be like this belt--completely useless**!*

- They forfeit God's favor.

Jeremiah 16:13
13** So I will throw you out of this land into a land neither you nor your fathers have known, and there you will serve other gods day and night, for **I will show you no favor.'

Jonah 2:8
***8** "Those who cling to worthless idols **forfeit the grace** that could be theirs.*

Ezekiel 5:11
***11** Therefore as surely as I live, declares the Sovereign LORD, because you have defiled my sanctuary with all your vile images and detestable practices, I myself will **withdraw my favor**; I will not look on you with pity or spare you.*

2 Chronicles 24:18-20
18** They abandoned the temple of the LORD, the God of their fathers, and worshiped Asherah poles and idols. Because of their guilt, God's anger came upon Judah and Jerusalem. **19
*Although the LORD sent prophets to the people to bring them back to him, and though they testified against them, they would not listen. **20** Then the Spirit of God came upon Zechariah son of Jehoiada the priest. He stood before the people and said, "This is what God says: 'Why do you disobey the LORD's commands?*

You will not prosper. Because you have forsaken the LORD, he has forsaken you. *' "*

- They become joined to idols; a union is formed.

Hosea 4:17
17 *Ephraim is* ***joined to idols****; leave him alone!*

Psalms 106:28
28 *They* ***yoked themselves to the Baal of Peor*** *and ate sacrifices offered to lifeless gods;*

- They become ignorant.

Isaiah 45:20
20 *"Gather together and come; assemble, you fugitives from the nations.* ***Ignorant*** *are those who carry about idols of wood, who pray to gods that cannot save.*

Jeremiah 10:8, 14
8 *They are all* ***senseless*** *and foolish; they are taught by worthless wooden idols.*

14 *Everyone is* ***senseless*** *and without knowledge; every goldsmith is shamed by his idols. His images are a fraud; they have no breath in them.*

- They increase their sorrows.

Psalms 16:4
4 *The* ***sorrows of those will increase*** *who run after other gods. I will not pour out their libations of blood or take up their names on my lips.*

- They may fear their gods (instead of fearing the Lord).

Isaiah 57:8-11
8** Behind your doors and your doorposts you have put your pagan symbols. Forsaking me, you uncovered your bed, you climbed into it and opened it wide; you made a pact with those whose beds you love, and you looked on their nakedness.* ***9** You went to Molech with olive oil and increased your perfumes. You sent your ambassadors far away; you descended to the grave itself!* ***10** You were wearied by all your ways, but you would not say, 'It is hopeless.' You found renewal of your strength, and so you did not faint.* ***11** "Whom have you so dreaded and feared* *that you have been false to me, and have neither remembered me nor pondered this in your hearts? Is it not because I have long been silent that* ***you do not fear me*?*

Psalms 96:4
4** For great is the LORD and most worthy of praise;* ***he is to be feared above all gods*.*

- They may boast in their idols.

Psalms 97:7
7 All who worship images are put to shame, those who ***boast in idols****-- worship him, all you gods!*

- Their hearts turn away from the Lord and become devoted to idols.

Deuteronomy 29:18
18** Make sure there is no man or woman, clan or tribe among you today whose* ***heart turns away from the LORD our God to go and worship the gods of those nations*; make sure there is no root among you that produces such bitter poison.*

Ezekiel 20:15-16
15 *Also with uplifted hand I swore to them in the desert that I would not bring them into the land I had given them--a land flowing with milk and honey, most beautiful of all lands--* ***16*** *because they rejected my laws and did not follow my decrees and desecrated my Sabbaths. For* ***their hearts were devoted to their idols****.*

1 Kings 11:9-10
9 *The LORD became angry with Solomon because* ***his heart had turned away from the LORD****, the God of Israel, who had appeared to him twice.* ***10*** *Although he had forbidden Solomon to follow other gods, Solomon did not keep the LORD's command.*

Ezekiel 14:1-4
1 *Some of the elders of Israel came to me and sat down in front of me.* ***2*** *Then the word of the LORD came to me:* ***3*** *"Son of man, these men have* ***set up idols in their hearts*** *and put wicked stumbling blocks before their faces. Should I let them inquire of me at all?* ***4*** *Therefore speak to them and tell them, 'This is what the Sovereign LORD says: When any Israelite* ***sets up idols in his heart*** *and puts a wicked stumbling block before his face and then goes to a prophet, I the LORD will answer him myself in keeping with his great idolatry.*

- They look to their idols.

Ezekiel 33:25
25 *Therefore say to them, 'This is what the Sovereign LORD says: Since you eat meat with the blood still in it and look to your idols and shed blood, should you then possess the land?*

- They consecrate themselves to their idols and become as vile as the idol they love.

Hosea 9:10
10 *"When I found Israel, it was like finding grapes in the desert; when I saw your fathers, it was like seeing the early fruit on the fig tree. But when they came to Baal Peor, they* ***consecrated themselves to that shameful idol*** *and* ***became as vile as the thing they loved****.*

- Their prosperity leads to more idolatry.

Hosea 10:1-2
1 *Israel was a spreading vine; he brought forth fruit for himself.* ***As his fruit increased, he built more altars; as his land prospered, he adorned his sacred stones****.* ***2*** *Their heart is deceitful, and now they must bear their guilt. The LORD will demolish their altars and destroy their sacred stones.*

- They stumble in their ways.

Jeremiah 18:15
15 *Yet my people have forgotten me; they burn incense to* ***worthless idols, which made them stumble in their ways*** *and in the ancient paths. They made them walk in bypaths and on roads not built up.*

- They become detestable.

Isaiah 41:22-24
22 *"Bring in [your idols] to tell us what is going to happen. Tell us what the former things were, so that we may consider them and know their final outcome. Or declare to us the things to come,* ***23*** *tell us what the future holds, so we may know that you are gods. Do something, whether good or bad, so that we*

will be dismayed and filled with fear. ***24*** *But you are less than nothing and your works are utterly worthless;* ***he who chooses you*** *[idols]* ***is detestable.***

- They trust in their idols and are turned back in shame.

Isaiah 42:17
17 *But those who trust in idols, who say to images, 'You are our gods,' will be turned back in utter shame.*

- They are defrauded.

Jeremiah 10:14
14 *Everyone is senseless and without knowledge; every goldsmith is shamed by his idols. His* ***images are a fraud; they have no breath in them****.*

Jeremiah 51:7
7 *"Every man is senseless and without knowledge; every goldsmith is shamed by his idols. His* ***images are a fraud; they have no breath in them****.*

Habakkuk 2:18-19
18 *"Of what value is an idol, since a man has carved it? Or an image that teaches lies? For he who makes it trusts in his own creation; he makes idols that* ***cannot speak****.* ***19*** *Woe to him who says to wood, 'Come to life!' Or to lifeless stone, 'Wake up!'* ***Can it give guidance?*** *It is covered with gold and silver;* ***there is no breath in it****.*

Isaiah 41:21-19
21 *"Present your case," says the LORD. "Set forth your arguments," says Jacob's King.* ***22 "Bring in [your idols] to tell us what is going to happen.*** *Tell us what the former things were, so that we may consider them and know their final outcome. Or*

declare to us the things to come, ***23*** *tell us what the future holds, so we may know that you are gods. Do something, whether good or bad, so that we will be dismayed and filled with fear.* ***24*** *But you are less than nothing and your works are utterly worthless; he who chooses you is detestable.* ***25*** *"I have stirred up one from the north, and he comes-- one from the rising sun who calls on my name. He treads on rulers as if they were mortar, as if he were a potter treading the clay.* ***26*** *Who told of this from the beginning, so we could know, or beforehand, so we could say, 'He was right'? No one told of this, no one foretold it, no one heard any words from you.* ***27*** *I was the first to tell Zion, 'Look, here they are!' I gave to Jerusalem a messenger of good tidings.* ***28*** *I look but there is no one-- no one among them to give counsel, no one to give answer when I ask them.* ***29 See, they are all false! Their deeds amount to nothing; their images are but wind and confusion.***

Zechariah 10:2
2 *The idols* ***speak deceit****, diviners* ***see visions that lie****; they* ***tell dreams that are false****, they give* ***comfort in vain****. Therefore the people wander like sheep oppressed for lack of a shepherd.*

- The silver and gold they use to make idols and images will not help them when God's wrath comes. The silver and gold only makes them stumble into sin.

Ezekiel 7:19-20
19 *They will throw their silver into the streets, and their gold will be an unclean thing.* ***Their silver and gold will not be able to save them in the day of the LORD's wrath****. They will not satisfy their hunger or fill their stomachs with it, for* ***it has made them stumble into sin. 20 They were proud of their beautiful jewelry and used it to make their detestable idols and vile images****. Therefore I will turn these into an unclean thing for them.*

- Their idolatry becomes tiring, but they find strength to pursue it anyway.

Isaiah 57:9-10
***9** You went to Molech with olive oil and increased your perfumes. You sent your ambassadors far away; you descended to the grave itself! **10** You were wearied by all your ways, but you would not say, 'It is hopeless.' You found renewal of your strength, and so you did not faint.*

Jeremiah 2:23-25
23** "How can you say, 'I am not defiled; I have not run after the Baals'? See how you behaved in the valley; consider what you have done. You are a swift she-camel running here and there, **24** a wild donkey accustomed to the desert, sniffing the wind in her craving-- in her heat who can restrain her? Any males that pursue her need not tire themselves; at mating time they will find her. 25 **Do not run until your feet are bare and your throat is dry. But you said, 'It's no use! I love foreign gods, and I must go after them.'

- They lack the wisdom to find the "opening of the womb" when the Lord brings deliverance from idolatry.

Hosea 13:1-13
***1** When Ephraim spoke, men trembled; he was exalted in Israel. But he became guilty of Baal worship and died. **2** Now they sin more and more; they make idols for themselves from their silver, cleverly fashioned images, all of them the work of craftsmen. It is said of these people, "They offer human sacrifice and kiss the calf-idols." **3** Therefore they will be like the morning mist, like the early dew that disappears, like chaff swirling from a threshing floor, like smoke escaping through a window. **4** "But I am the LORD your God, [who brought you] out of Egypt. You shall acknowledge no God but me, no Savior except me. **5** I cared*

for you in the desert, in the land of burning heat. ***6*** *When I fed them, they were satisfied; when they were satisfied, they became proud; then they forgot me.* ***7*** *So I will come upon them like a lion, like a leopard I will lurk by the path.* ***8*** *Like a bear robbed of her cubs, I will attack them and rip them open. Like a lion I will devour them; a wild animal will tear them apart.* ***9*** *"You are destroyed, O Israel, because you are against me, against your helper.* ***10*** *Where is your king, that he may save you? Where are your rulers in all your towns, of whom you said, 'Give me a king and princes'?* ***11*** *So in my anger I gave you a king, and in my wrath I took him away.* ***12*** *The guilt of Ephraim is stored up, his sins are kept on record. 13* ***Pains as of a woman in childbirth come to him, but he is a child without wisdom; when the time arrives, he does not come to the opening of the womb.***

- They try to hide their idolatry from the Lord.

2 Kings 17:7-12
7 All this took place because the Israelites had sinned against the LORD their God, who had brought them up out of Egypt from under the power of Pharaoh king of Egypt. They worshiped other gods ***8*** *and followed the practices of the nations the LORD had driven out before them, as well as the practices that the kings of Israel had introduced.* ***9*** *The* ***Israelites secretly did things*** *against the LORD their God that were not right. From watchtower to fortified city they built themselves high places in all their towns.* ***10*** *They set up sacred stones and Asherah poles on every high hill and under every spreading tree.* ***11*** *At every high place they burned incense, as the nations whom the LORD had driven out before them had done. They did wicked things that provoked the LORD to anger.* ***12*** *They worshiped idols, though the LORD had said, "You shall not do this."*

Ezekiel 8:12
***12** He said to me, "Son of man, have you seen what the elders of the house of Israel are doing in the darkness, each at the shrine of his own idol? They say, **'The LORD does not see us**; the LORD has forsaken the land.' "*

Jeremiah 16:17-18
***17 My eyes are on all their ways; they are not hidden from me, nor is their sin concealed from my eyes. 18** I will repay them double for their wickedness and their sin, because they have defiled my land with the lifeless forms of their vile images and have filled my inheritance with their detestable idols."*

- They sell themselves to do evil.

2 Kings 17:16-17
***16** They forsook all the commands of the LORD their God and made for themselves two idols cast in the shape of calves, and an Asherah pole. They bowed down to all the starry hosts, and they worshiped Baal. **17** They sacrificed their sons and daughters in the fire. They practiced divination and sorcery and **sold themselves to do evil** in the eyes of the LORD, provoking him to anger.*

Hosea 8:9
9** For they have gone up to Assyria like a wild donkey wandering alone. Ephraim has **sold herself to lovers.

- They embrace their gods.

1 Kings 9:9
***9** People will answer, 'Because they have forsaken the LORD their God, who brought their fathers out of Egypt, and have **embraced other gods**, worshiping and serving them--that is why the LORD brought all this disaster on them.' "*

- They become like their idols in that they cannot speak, see, hear, talk, smell, feel, or walk.

Psalms 135:15-18
15** The idols of the nations are silver and gold, made by the hands of men. **16** They have mouths, but **cannot speak**, eyes, but they **cannot see; 17** they have ears, but **cannot hear**, nor is there breath in their mouths. **18 Those who make them will be like them, and so will all who trust in them.

Psalms 115:4-8
***4** But their idols are silver and gold, made by the hands of men. **5** They have mouths, but **cannot speak**, eyes, but they **cannot see; 6** they have ears, but **cannot hear,** noses, but they **cannot smell; 7** they have hands, but **cannot feel**, feet, but they **cannot walk**; nor can they utter a sound with their throats. **8 Those who make them will be like them, and so will all who trust in them**.*

- They become defenseless to their enemies, because the Lord hands them over.

Judges 2:12-15
***12** They forsook the LORD, the God of their fathers, who had brought them out of Egypt. They followed and worshiped various gods of the peoples around them. They provoked the LORD to anger **13** because they forsook him and served Baal and the Ashtoreths. **14** In his anger against Israel the LORD handed them over to raiders who plundered them. He sold them to their enemies all around, whom **they were no longer able to resist**. **15** Whenever Israel went out to fight, the hand of the LORD was against them to defeat them, just as he had sworn to them. They were in great distress.*

- They forgot God, and deserted him for idols.

Jeremiah 13:25
25 *This is your lot, the portion I have decreed for you," declares*
the LORD, "because ***you have forgotten me and trusted in***
false gods*.*

Hosea 4:10-12
10 *"They will eat but not have enough; they will engage in pros-*
titution but not increase, because they have ***deserted the LORD***
to give themselves 11 to prostitution*, to old wine and new, which*
take away the understanding ***12*** *of my people.* ***They consult a***
wooden idol and are answered by a stick of wood. A spirit of
prostitution leads them astray; they are unfaithful to their God*.*

Isaiah 57:6-9
6 *[The idols] among the smooth stones of the ravines are your*
portion; they, they are your lot. Yes, to them you have poured
out drink offerings and offered grain offerings. In the light of
these things, should I relent? ***7*** *You have made your bed on a*
high and lofty hill; there you went up to offer your sacrifices. ***8***
Behind your doors and your doorposts you have put your pagan
symbols. ***Forsaking me, you uncovered your bed****, you climbed*
into it and opened it wide; you made a pact with those whose
beds you love, and you looked on their nakedness. ***9*** *You went*
to Molech with olive oil and increased your perfumes. You sent
your ambassadors far away; you descended to the grave itself!

Judges 10:11-14
11 *The LORD replied, "When the Egyptians, the Amorites, the*
Ammonites, the Philistines, ***12*** *the Sidonians, the Amalekites and*
the Maonites oppressed you and you cried to me for help, did I
not save you from their hands? ***13*** *But* ***you have forsaken me***
and served other gods*, so I will no longer save you.* ***14*** *Go and*

cry out to the gods you have chosen. Let them save you when you are in trouble!"

1 Kings 9:9

9 *You have done more evil than all who lived before you. You have made for yourself other gods, idols made of metal; you have provoked me to anger and* ***thrust me behind your back****.*

Ezekiel 14:5

5 *I will do this to recapture the hearts of the people of Israel, who have all* ***deserted me for their idols****.*

1 Samuel 8:8

8 *As they have done from the day I brought them up out of Egypt until this day,* ***forsaking me and serving other gods,*** *so they are doing to you.*

Jeremiah 2:9-12

9 *"Therefore I bring charges against you again," declares the LORD. "And I will bring charges against your children's children.* ***10*** *Cross over to the coasts of Kittim and look, send to Kedar and observe closely; see if there has ever been anything like this:* ***11*** *Has a nation ever changed its gods? (Yet they are not gods at all.) But my people have* ***exchanged their Glory for worthless idols****.* ***12*** *Be appalled at this, O heavens, and shudder with great horror," declares the LORD.*

Psalms 106:19-21

19 *At Horeb they made a calf and worshiped an idol cast from metal.* ***20*** *They* ***exchanged their Glory for an image of a bull****, which eats grass.* ***21*** *They* ***forgot the God*** *who saved them, who had done great things in Egypt,*

- Their spiritual blindness became enormous.

Jeremiah 7:9-10
9 *" 'Will you steal and murder, commit adultery and perjury, burn incense to Baal and follow other gods you have not known,* ***10*** *and then come and stand before me in this house, which bears my Name, and say,* ***"We are safe"--safe to do all these detestable things****?*

Jeremiah 11:15
15 *"What is my beloved doing in my temple as she works out her evil schemes with many?* ***Can consecrated meat avert [your punishment]****? When you engage in your wickedness, then you rejoice."*

Jeremiah 44:17-18
17 *We will certainly do everything we said we would: We will burn incense to the Queen of Heaven and will pour out drink offerings to her just as we and our fathers, our kings and our officials did in the towns of Judah and in the streets of Jerusalem. At that time we had plenty of food and were well off and suffered no harm.* ***18*** *But* ***ever since we stopped burning incense to the Queen of Heaven and pouring out drink offerings to her, we have had nothing and have been perishing by sword and famine."***

Ezekiel 18:25-32
25 "Yet you say, 'The way of the Lord is not just*.' Hear, O house of Israel: Is my way unjust? Is it not your ways that are unjust?*
26 *If a righteous man turns from his righteousness and commits sin, he will die for it; because of the sin he has committed he will die.* ***27*** *But if a wicked man turns away from the wickedness he has committed and does what is just and right, he will save his life.* ***28*** *Because he considers all the offenses he has committed and turns away from them, he will surely live; he will not die.*

29 Yet the house of Israel says, 'The way of the Lord is not just.'
Are my ways unjust, O house of Israel? Is it not your ways that
are unjust? **30** "Therefore, O house of Israel, I will judge you,
each one according to his ways, declares the Sovereign LORD.
Repent! Turn away from all your offenses; then sin will not be
your downfall. **31** Rid yourselves of all the offenses you have
committed, and get a new heart and a new spirit. Why will you
die, O house of Israel? **32** For I take no pleasure in the death of
anyone, declares the Sovereign LORD. Repent and live!

Hosea 2:5-8
5 Their mother has been unfaithful and has conceived them
in disgrace. She said, **'I will go after my lovers, who give me
my food and my water, my wool and my linen, my oil and my
drink.'** **6** Therefore I will block her path with thornbushes; I will
wall her in so that she cannot find her way. **7** She will chase after
her lovers but not catch them; she will look for them but not find
them. Then she will say, 'I will go back to my husband as at first,
for then I was better off than now.' **8 She has not acknowledged
that I was the one who gave her the grain, the new wine and
oil, who lavished on her the silver and gold**-- which they used
for Baal

Hosea 11:3
1 "When Israel was a child, I loved him, and out of Egypt I called
my son. **2** But the more I called Israel, the further they went
from me. They sacrificed to the Baals and they burned incense
to images. **3** It was I who taught Ephraim to walk, taking them
by the arms; but **they did not realize it was I who healed them.**

Ezekiel 20:31
31 When you offer your gifts--the sacrifice of your sons in the
fire--you continue to defile yourselves with all your idols to
this day. **Am I to let you inquire of me,** O house of Israel? As

surely as I live, declares the Sovereign LORD, ***I will not let you inquire of me.***

2 Chronicles 25:14-15
14 *When Amaziah returned from slaughtering the Edomites, he brought back the gods of the people of Seir. He set them up as his own gods, bowed down to them and burned sacrifices to them.*
15 *The anger of the LORD burned against Amaziah, and he sent a prophet to him, who said, "**Why do you consult this people's gods, which could not save their own people from your hand?**"*

2 Chronicles 28:22-23
22 *In his time of trouble King Ahaz became even more unfaithful to the LORD.* ***23*** *He offered sacrifices to the gods of Damascus, who had defeated him; for he thought, "**Since the gods of the kings of Aram have helped them, I will sacrifice to them so they will help me.**" But they were his downfall and the downfall of all Israel.*

Jeremiah 2:26-27
26 *"As a thief is disgraced when he is caught, so the house of Israel is disgraced-- they, their kings and their officials, their priests and their prophets.* ***27 They say to wood, 'You are my father,' and to stone, 'You gave me birth.'*** *They have turned their backs to me and not their faces; yet when they are in trouble, they say, 'Come and save us!'*

Jeremiah 3:6-9
6 *During the reign of King Josiah, the LORD said to me, "Have you seen what faithless Israel has done? She has gone up on every high hill and under every spreading tree and has committed adultery there.* ***7*** *I thought that after she had done all this she would return to me but she did not, and her unfaithful sister Judah saw it.* ***8*** *I gave faithless Israel her certificate of divorce and sent her away because of all her adulteries. Yet* ***I saw that***

her unfaithful sister Judah had no fear; she also went out and committed adultery. 9 *Because Israel's immorality mattered so little to her, she defiled the land and committed adultery with stone and wood.*

Jeremiah 2:23-24

23 "How can you say, 'I am not defiled; I have not run after the Baals'*? See how you behaved in the valley; consider what you have done. You are a swift she-camel running here and there,*
24 *a wild donkey accustomed to the desert, sniffing the wind in her craving-- in her heat who can restrain her? Any males that pursue her need not tire themselves; at mating time they will find her.*

Jeremiah 2:29

29 "Why do you bring charges against me? You have all rebelled against me,*" declares the LORD.*

Jeremiah 2:31-35

31 *"You of this generation, consider the word of the LORD: "Have I been a desert to Israel or a land of great darkness? Why do my people say, 'We are free to roam; we will come to you no more'?* ***32*** *Does a maiden forget her jewelry, a bride her wedding ornaments? Yet my people have forgotten me, days without number.* ***33*** *How skilled you are at pursuing love! Even the worst of women can learn from your ways.* ***34*** *On your clothes men find the lifeblood of the innocent poor, though you did not catch them breaking in. Yet in spite of all this* ***35*** *you say,* ***'I am innocent; he is not angry with me.' But I will pass judgment on you because you say, 'I have not sinned.****'*

Hosea 8:11

11 "Though Ephraim built many altars for sin offerings, these have become altars for sinning*.*

WHAT HAPPENS TO THOSE WHO HAVE GREED?

Which, if any, of these do you think might happen to those who have greed?

They harm themselves by their greed.

They defile the land, the city, and themselves by their greed.

God gives them over to a stubborn heart because of their greed.

They desecrate or defile the sanctuary the Lord loves by their greed.

They became enslaved by their greed.

They are led astray by their greed.

They become cursed because of their greed.

They want to get away from the Lord because of their greed.

They become useless (and may feel useless) because of their greed.

They forfeit God's favor because of their greed.

They become joined to greed.

They become ignorant because of their greed.

They increase their sorrows because of their greed.

They may show respect to their greed (instead of fearing the Lord).

They may boast in their greed.

Their hearts turn away from the Lord and become devoted to greed.

They look to their greed.

They consecrate themselves to their greed and become as vile as the greed they love.

Their prosperity leads to more greed.

They stumble in their ways because of their greed.

They become detestable because of their greed.

They trust in their greed and are turned back in shame.

They are defrauded by their greed.

The silver and gold they use to support their greed will not help them when God's wrath comes. The silver and gold only makes them stumble into sin.

Their greed becomes tiring, but they find strength to pursue it anyway.

They lack the wisdom to find the opening of the womb when the Lord brings deliverance from their greed.

They try to hide their greed from the Lord.

They sell themselves to do evil for greed.

They embrace the gods behind their greed.

They become like their greed in that they cannot speak, see, hear, talk, smell, feel, or walk.

They become defenseless to their enemies because the Lord hands them over.

They forget God, and desert him for greed.

Their spiritual blindness becomes enormous.

- They believe they can be greedy and come to God and say we are safe to do this.
- They believe the fruit of their greed will protect them from the Lord's judgment.
- They believe they were well off when greedy, and whenever they tried to stop they believed they had nothing, so they went back to greed.

- They believe the Lord is unjust to hold them accountable for greed.
- They believe they were better off with their greed than now when they gave it up.
- They find it is difficult to see the Lord as father and healer.
- They find it difficult to inquire of the Lord, because he does not answer, and they we do not know why.
- They believe the sacrifices they made out of greed were for their children.
- Others have prospered because of their greed, so why not us?
- Those Israelites were awfully stupid for their idolatry; our greed is not comparable.
- We are not defiled by our greed.
- It is not right that the Lord should interfere with our greed.
- We are free to pursue greed; it is our right. God does not have the right to be upset about this.
- The altars we built for God by our greed are good. How can God call them altars for sinning?

THE TENACITY OF IDOLATRY

We will find that idolatry had an immense tenacity among God's people under the Old Covenant. The word tenacity means it was very, very difficult to get rid of. (This will be helpful in understanding the immense tenacity of greed among God's people under the New Covenant.)

The Old Covenant which included prohibition of idolatry (*Exodus 20:4*) was given after the Israelites were delivered out of slavery to Egypt, in particular 3 months after they left Egypt at Mount Sinai (*Exodus 19* and *20*). We will look at the tenacity of idolatry in several periods of their history. As a reminder, the Israelites descended from Abram (later called Abraham) as follows: Abram had a son called Isaac who had a son called Jacob. Jacob's name was changed by God to Israel, the father of the 12 tribes (headed by the 12 sons) of Israel – the Israelites.

<u>Tenacity of Idolatry BEFORE the Covenant was declared by God to the Israelites.</u>

There are two mentions of idolatry before the 70 Israelites (Jacob's descendants) entered Egypt.

a. Terah, the father of Abraham and his brother Nahor, worshipped idols in Terah's land (*Joshua 24:2*).

b. One of Jacob's two wives, Rachel, stole the household gods of her father Laban who had descended from Nahor (*Genesis 31:31-35),* so Jacob's wife Rachel worshipped the idols of her father, a practice that may have come down from her ancestor -- great, great grandfather Terah who worshipped idols.

When Israel entered Egypt there were 70 of them. They carried the idols of Terah's land into Egypt with them (*Joshua 24:14)*. They were in Egypt 430 years, in the beginning they were free and later were made slaves. By the time they left Egypt the Israelites had expanded to about 600,000 adult men on foot (*Exodus 12:37),* or roughly 2,000,000 people including women and children. When they were in Egypt, God revealed himself to them and told the people to get rid of the vile images they set their eyes on, and to not defile themselves with the idols of Egypt. But they would not listen and they did not get rid of the vile images they set their eyes on, nor did they forsake the idols of Egypt (*Ezekiel 20:5-10)*. They were also offering sacrifices to goat idols (*Leviticus 17:7)*. This was all while they were in Egypt.

The Israelites carried both the idols of Terah's land and the idols of Egypt -- out of Egypt with them (*Joshua 24:14),* later through 40 years in the desert, into Canaan for about 30 years, up to the time when Joshua retires from leading the people (*Joshua 24:14)*. Note that they carried the idols of the gods of Egypt with them, even though they saw the 10 judgments of God on the gods of Egypt (*Numbers 33:4)*.

So we know that when the people stand before Mount Sinai to receive the Covenant from God they have idols in their possession from both Egypt and Terah's land.

Tenacity of Idolatry AFTER the Covenant was declared by God to the Israelites UP TO the death of King Solomon.

The Covenant was given at Mount Sinai and it stipulated that God's people were to not make, bow down, or worship idols. However, before the Israelites even left Mount Sinai the following happens.

Exodus 32:1-4
1 *When the people saw that Moses was so long in coming down from the mountain, they gathered around Aaron and said, "Come, make us gods who will go before us. As for this fellow Moses who brought us up out of Egypt, we don't know what has happened to him."* ***2*** *Aaron answered them, "Take off the gold earrings that your wives, your sons and your daughters are wearing, and bring them to me."* ***3*** *So all the people took off their earrings and brought them to Aaron.* ***4*** *He took what they handed him and* ***made it into an idol*** *cast in the shape of a calf, fashioning it with a tool.* ***Then they said, "These are your gods, O Israel, who brought you up out of Egypt."***

After Mount Sinai the Israelites travel up to the land of Canaan, but due to fear of the giants in Canaan they refuse to enter and want to choose a leader and go back to Egypt. Instead they spend 40 years wandering in the desert. The roughly 2,000,000 Israelites still have the idols of Terah's land and of Egypt with them during the 40 years with Moses leading them (*Joshua 24:14*); they probably hid them from Moses.

At the end of the 40 years in the desert, they travel to the plains of Moab and camp along the Jordan across from Jericho (part of the land of Canaan). The king of Moab gets scared of the Israelites and devises a plan to hire Balaam to curse Israel; the plan fails when Balaam blesses them and forfeits his fee. However, Balaam who loved the wages of wickedness (*2 Peter*

2:15) devises a plan himself (*Numbers 31:15-16*). He advises the women of Midian to have the Israelite men enter into sexual immorality and then get invited to the sacrifices of their gods so the Israelites would turn away from the Lord's and his anger would burn against them. This plan worked (*Numbers 25:1-9*). This sin, worship of the Baal of Peor, plagued Israel for years (*Joshua 22:17*). Not only that, this evil plan was implemented at Pergamum and Thyatira during the early church (*Revelation 2:14, 20*).

Before entering the land of Canaan, Moses reiterates the Law on idolatry, including severe penalties (death) for idolatry. *Deuteronomy 4:3, 15-19, 23-28, 34; 5:7, 8; 6:14-15; 7:3-6, 25-26; 9:4-6; 11:16-21; 12:2-4, 29-31; 13:1-18; 16:21-22; 27:15; 28:36, 64; 31:16, 20; 32:16-17, 21, 37-38.*

Yet the people carried the idols of Terah's land and of Egypt into Canaan (*Joshua 24:14*). Worse, they did not break down all the altars of the people who lived in Canaan and allowed some of those people to live (*Judges 2:1-2*), contrary to what the Lord had commanded. The tenacity of idolatry during the period of the Judges is summarized below in *Judges 2:10-23, 3:5-6*. There were numerous cycles of idolatry, God puts them in captivity, they call to God, God sends a judge who delivers them and judges them for a period, the judge dies, the people return to idolatry. This went on for over 350 years (assumes I calculated right.)

> *Judges 2:10-23*
> ***10*** *After that whole generation [Joshua's generation] had been gathered to their fathers, another generation grew up, who knew neither the LORD nor what he had done for Israel.* ***11*** *Then the Israelites did evil in the eyes of the LORD and served the Baals.* ***12*** *They forsook the LORD,*

the God of their fathers, who had brought them
out of Egypt. They followed and worshiped var-
ious gods of the peoples around them. They pro-
voked the LORD to anger **13** *because they forsook*
him and served Baal and the Ashtoreths. **14** *In*
his anger against Israel the LORD handed them
over to raiders who plundered them. He sold them
to their enemies all around, whom they were no
longer able to resist. **15** *Whenever Israel went out*
to fight, the hand of the LORD was against them
to defeat them, just as he had sworn to them. They
were in great distress. **16** *Then the LORD raised*
up judges, who saved them out of the hands of
these raiders. **17** *Yet they would not listen to their*
judges but prostituted themselves to other gods
and worshiped them. Unlike their fathers, they
quickly turned from the way in which their fathers
had walked, the way of obedience to the LORD's
commands. **18** *Whenever the LORD raised up a*
judge for them, he was with the judge and saved
them out of the hands of their enemies as long as
the judge lived; for the LORD had compassion on
them as they groaned under those who oppressed
and afflicted them. **19** *But when the judge died,*
the people returned to ways even more corrupt
than those of their fathers, following other gods
and serving and worshiping them. They refused to
give up their evil practices and stubborn ways. **20**
Therefore the LORD was very angry with Israel
and said, "Because this nation has violated the
covenant that I laid down for their forefathers and
has not listened to me, **21** *I will no longer drive*
out before them any of the nations Joshua left
when he died. **22** *I will use them to test Israel and*
see whether they will keep the way of the LORD

and walk in it as their forefathers did." ***23*** *The LORD had allowed those nations to remain; he did not drive them out at once by giving them into the hands of Joshua.*

Judges 3:5-6
5 *The Israelites lived among the Canaanites, Hittites, Amorites, Perizzites, Hivites and Jebusites.* ***6*** *They took their daughters in marriage and gave their own daughters to their sons, and served their gods.*

We then have the last judge, Samuel, which then leads into the period of the kings of all Israel (all 12 tribes): Saul (42 years), David (40 years) and Solomon (40 years).

During Samuel's years, we find him saying to Israel,

1 Samuel 7:3-4
3 *And Samuel said to the whole house of Israel, "If you are returning to the LORD with all your hearts, then rid yourselves of the foreign gods and the Ashtoreths and commit yourselves to the LORD and serve him only, and he will deliver you out of the hand of the Philistines."* ***4*** *So the Israelites put away their Baals and Ashtoreths, and served the LORD only.*

Yet when Samuel grew old we find the LORD saying:

1 Samuel 8:6-8
6 *But when they said, "Give us a king to lead us," this displeased Samuel; so he prayed to the LORD.* ***7*** *And the LORD told him: "Listen to all that the people are saying to you; it is not you they*

> *have rejected, but they have rejected me as their king.* ***8*** *As they have done from the day I brought them up out of Egypt* ***until this day, forsaking me and serving other gods****, so they are doing to you.*

Saul, King of Israel, had serious problems, but idolatry did not appear to be one of them.

David, King of Israel, did not worship idols and his heart was committed to worship the Lord alone. There are indications in some of David's Psalms that idolatry was taking place (*Psalms 4:2; 16:4; 31:6)*. However, Isaiah refers to a time of Jerusalem when the city was full of justice, righteousness, and faithfulness (*Isaiah 1:21)* which can only refer to David's reign.

In one sense the tenacity of idolatry ceased or was greatly reduced during David's reign, but then came back during Solomon's reign.

In spite of Solomon's wisdom and great wealth, and his building the Temple where God would meet with the people, Solomon made alliances with surrounding nations that included marrying women from those nations, leading him to worship the gods of those wives. He married foreign wives who turned his heart after other gods. God responded by declaring he would tear the kingdom away from Solomon and give it to his subordinate, except for one tribe Judah which held Jerusalem and the Temple for David's sake.

> *1 Kings 11:1-13*
> ***1*** *King Solomon, however, loved many foreign women besides Pharaoh's daughter--Moabites, Ammonites, Edomites, Sidonians and Hittites.* ***2***
> *They were from nations about which the LORD had told the Israelites, "You must not intermarry*

with them, because they will surely turn your hearts after their gods." Nevertheless, Solomon held fast to them in love. ***3*** *He had seven hundred wives of royal birth and three hundred concubines, and his wives led him astray.* ***4*** *As Solomon grew old, his wives turned his heart after other gods, and his heart was not fully devoted to the LORD his God, as the heart of David his father had been.* ***5*** *He followed Ashtoreth the goddess of the Sidonians, and Molech the detestable god of the Ammonites.* ***6*** *So Solomon did evil in the eyes of the LORD; he did not follow the LORD completely, as David his father had done.* ***7*** *On a hill east of Jerusalem, Solomon built a high place for Chemosh the detestable god of Moab, and for Molech the detestable god of the Ammonites.* ***8*** *He did the same for all his foreign wives, who burned incense and offered sacrifices to their gods.* ***9*** *The LORD became angry with Solomon because his heart had turned away from the LORD, the God of Israel, who had appeared to him twice.* ***10*** *Although he had forbidden Solomon to follow other gods, Solomon did not keep the LORD's command.* ***11*** *So the LORD said to Solomon, "Since this is your attitude and you have not kept my covenant and my decrees, which I commanded you, I will most certainly tear the kingdom away from you and give it to one of your subordinates.* ***12*** *Nevertheless, for the sake of David your father, I will not do it during your lifetime. I will tear it out of the hand of your son.* ***13*** *Yet I will not tear the whole kingdom from him, but will give him one tribe for the sake of David my servant and for the sake of Jerusalem, which I have chosen."*

Tenacity of Idolatry of Israel (10 northern tribes) AFTER Solomon died UP TO the exile of the 10 northern tribes now called Israel or Ephraim and sometimes called Samaria

Jeroboam (king of Israel for 22 years)

I Kings 12:28-33
28 *After seeking advice, the king made two golden calves. He said to the people, "It is too much for you to go up to Jerusalem. Here are your gods, O Israel, who brought you up out of Egypt."* **29** *One he set up in Bethel, and the other in Dan.* **30** *And this thing became a sin; the people went even as far as Dan to worship the one there.* **31** *Jeroboam built shrines on high places and appointed priests from all sorts of people, even though they were not Levites.* **32** *He instituted a festival on the fifteenth day of the eighth month, like the festival held in Judah, and offered sacrifices on the altar. This he did in Bethel, sacrificing to the calves he had made. And at Bethel he also installed priests at the high places he had made.* **33** *On the fifteenth day of the eighth month, a month of his own choosing, he offered sacrifices on the altar he had built at Bethel. So he instituted the festival for the Israelites and went up to the altar to make offerings.*

1 Kings 13:33-34
33 *Even after this, Jeroboam did not change his evil ways, but once more appointed priests for the high places from all sorts of people. Anyone who wanted to become a priest he consecrated for the high places.* **34** *This was the sin of the house of Jeroboam that led to its downfall and to its destruction from the face of the earth.*

Nadab (king of Israel for 2 years)

1 Kings 15:26
***26** He did evil in the eyes of the LORD, walking in the ways of his father and in his sin, which he had caused Israel to commit.*

Baasha (king of Israel for 24 years)

1 Kings 15:34
***34** He did evil in the eyes of the LORD, walking in the ways of Jeroboam and in his sin, which he had caused Israel to commit.*

Elah (king of Israel for 2 years)

1 Kings 16:12-13
***12** So Zimri destroyed the whole family of Baasha, in accordance with the word of the LORD spoken against Baasha through the prophet Jehu-- **13** because of all the sins Baasha and his son Elah had committed and had caused Israel to commit, so that they provoked the LORD, the God of Israel, to anger by their worthless idols.*

Zimri (king of Israel for 7 days)

1 Kings 16:18-19
***18** When Zimri saw that the city was taken, he went into the citadel of the royal palace and set the palace on fire around him. So he died, **19** because of the sins he had committed, doing evil in the eyes of the LORD and walking in the ways of Jeroboam and in the sin he had committed and had caused Israel to commit.*

<u>Omri (king of Israel for 12 years)</u>

<u>1 Kings 16:24-26</u>
24 *He bought the hill of Samaria from Shemer for two talents of silver and built a city on the hill, calling it Samaria, after Shemer, the name of the former owner of the hill.* ***25*** *But Omri did evil in the eyes of the LORD and sinned more than all those before him.* ***26*** *He walked in all the ways of Jeroboam son of Nebat and in his sin, which he had caused Israel to commit, so that they provoked the LORD, the God of Israel, to anger by their worthless idols.*

<u>Ahab (king of Israel for 22 years)</u>

<u>1 Kings 16:30-33</u>
30 *Ahab son of Omri did more evil in the eyes of the LORD than any of those before him.* ***31*** *He not only considered it trivial to commit the sins of Jeroboam son of Nebat, but he also married Jezebel daughter of Ethbaal king of the Sidonians, and began to serve Baal and worship him.* ***32*** *He set up an altar for Baal in the temple of Baal that he built in Samaria.*
33 *Ahab also made an Asherah pole and did more to provoke the LORD, the God of Israel, to anger than did all the kings of Israel before him.*

Prophet Elijah active against idolatry

<u>Ahaziah (king of Israel for 2 years)</u>

<u>1 Kings 22:52-53</u>
52 *He did evil in the eyes of the LORD, because he walked in the ways of his father and mother*

and in the ways of Jeroboam son of Nebat, who caused Israel to sin. ***53*** *He served and worshiped Baal and provoked the LORD, the God of Israel, to anger, just as his father had done.*

Joram (king of Israel for 12 years)

2 Kings 3:2-3
2 He did evil in the eyes of the LORD, but not as his father and mother had done. He got rid of the sacred stone of Baal that his father had made. ***3***
Nevertheless he clung to the sins of Jeroboam son of Nebat, which he had caused Israel to commit; he did not turn away from them.

Elijah is taken up and the prophet Elisha active against idolatry

Jehu (king of Israel for 28 years)

2 Kings 9:6-10
6 *Jehu got up and went into the house. Then the prophet poured the oil on Jehu's head and declared, "This is what the LORD, the God of Israel, says: 'I anoint you king over the LORD's people Israel.* ***7*** *You are to destroy the house of Ahab your master, and I will avenge the blood of my servants the prophets and the blood of all the LORD's servants shed by Jezebel.* ***8*** *The whole house of Ahab will perish. I will cut off from Ahab every last male in Israel--slave or free.*
9 *I will make the house of Ahab like the house of Jeroboam son of Nebat and like the house of Baasha son of Ahijah.* ***10*** *As for Jezebel, dogs will devour her on the plot of ground at Jezreel,*

and no one will bury her.' " Then he opened the door and ran.

2 Kings 10:30-31
***30** The LORD said to Jehu, "Because you have done well in accomplishing what is right in my eyes and have done to the house of Ahab all I had in mind to do, your descendants will sit on the throne of Israel to the fourth generation."*
***31** Yet Jehu was not careful to keep the law of the LORD, the God of Israel, with all his heart. He did not turn away from the sins of Jeroboam, which he had caused Israel to commit.*

<u>Jehoahaz (king of Israel for 17 years)</u>

<u>2 Kings 13:2-6</u>
***2** He did evil in the eyes of the LORD by following the sins of Jeroboam son of Nebat, which he had caused Israel to commit, and he did not turn away from them.*
***3** So the LORD's anger burned against Israel, and for a long time he kept them under the power of Hazael king of Aram and Ben-Hadad his son.*
***4** Then Jehoahaz sought the LORD's favor, and the LORD listened to him, for he saw how severely the king of Aram was oppressing Israel.*
***5** The LORD provided a deliverer for Israel, and they escaped from the power of Aram. So the Israelites lived in their own homes as they had before.*
***6** But they did not turn away from the sins of the house of Jeroboam, which he had caused Israel to commit; they continued in them. Also, the Asherah pole remained standing in Samaria.*

Jehoash (king of Israel for 16 years)

2 Kings 13:11
***11** He did evil in the eyes of the LORD and did not turn away from any of the sins of Jeroboam son of Nebat, which he had caused Israel to commit; he continued in them.*

Jeroboam II (king of Israel for 41 years)

2 Kings 14:24
***24** He did evil in the eyes of the LORD and did not turn away from any of the sins of Jeroboam son of Nebat, which he had caused Israel to commit.*

Elisha the prophet dies.

The prophet Amos speaks against injustice and idolatry.

The prophet Hosea speaks against idolatry.

Zechariah (king of Israel for 6 months)

2 Kings 15:9
***9** He did evil in the eyes of the LORD, as his fathers had done. He did not turn away from the sins of Jeroboam son of Nebat, which he had caused Israel to commit.*

Shallum (king of Israel for 1 month)

Menahem (king of Israel for 10 years)

2 Kings 15:18
***18** He did evil in the eyes of the LORD. During his entire reign he did not turn away from the sins of Jeroboam son of Nebat, which he had caused Israel to commit.*

Pekahiah (king of Israel for 2 years)

2 Kings 15:24
***24** Pekahiah did evil in the eyes of the LORD. He did not turn away from the sins of Jeroboam son of Nebat, which he had caused Israel to commit.*

Pekah (king of Israel for 22 years)

2 Kings 15:28
***28** He did evil in the eyes of the LORD. He did not turn away from the sins of Jeroboam son of Nebat, which he had caused Israel to commit.*

Hoshea (last king of Israel, 9 years)

2 Kings 17:2
***2** He did evil in the eyes of the LORD, but not like the kings of Israel who preceded him.*

2 Kings 17:3-6
***3** Shalmaneser king of Assyria came up to attack Hoshea, who had been Shalmaneser's vassal and had paid him tribute. **4** But the king of Assyria discovered that Hoshea was a traitor, for he had sent envoys to So king of Egypt, and he no longer paid tribute to the king of Assyria, as he had done year by year. Therefore Shalmaneser seized him and put him in prison. **5** The king of Assyria invaded*

the entire land, marched against Samaria and laid siege to it for three years. ***6*** *In the ninth year of Hoshea, the king of Assyria captured Samaria and deported the Israelites to Assyria. He settled them in Halah, in Gozan on the Habor River and in the towns of the Medes.*

Reasons for the deportation of Israel (10 northern tribes) by Assyria.

2 Kings 17:7-23
7 *All this took place because the Israelites had sinned against the LORD their God, who had brought them up out of Egypt from under the power of Pharaoh king of Egypt.* ***They worshiped other gods*** *8* ***and followed the practices of the nations the LORD had driven out before them, as well as the practices that the kings of Israel had introduced. 9*** *The Israelites secretly did things against the LORD their God that were not right. From watchtower to fortified city they built themselves high places in all their towns.* ***10*** *They set up sacred stones and Asherah poles on every high hill and under every spreading tree.* ***11*** *At every high place they burned incense, as the nations whom the LORD had driven out before them had done. They did wicked things that provoked the LORD to anger.* ***12*** *They worshiped idols, though the LORD had said, "You shall not do this."* ***13*** *The LORD warned Israel and Judah through all his prophets and seers: "Turn from your evil ways. Observe my commands and decrees, in accordance with the entire Law that I commanded your fathers to obey and that I delivered to you through my servants the prophets."* ***14*** *But they would not listen and*

were as stiff-necked as their fathers, who did not trust in the LORD their God. ***15*** *They rejected his decrees and the covenant he had made with their fathers and the warnings he had given them. They followed worthless idols and themselves became worthless. They imitated the nations around them although the LORD had ordered them, "Do not do as they do," and they did the things the LORD had forbidden them to do.* ***16*** *They forsook all the commands of the LORD their God and made for themselves two idols cast in the shape of calves, and an Asherah pole. They bowed down to all the starry hosts, and they worshiped Baal.* ***17*** *They sacrificed their sons and daughters in the fire. They practiced divination and sorcery and sold themselves to do evil in the eyes of the LORD, provoking him to anger.* ***18*** *So the LORD was very angry with Israel and removed them from his presence. Only the tribe of Judah was left,* ***19*** *and even Judah did not keep the commands of the LORD their God. They followed the practices Israel had introduced.* ***20*** *Therefore the LORD rejected all the people of Israel; he afflicted them and gave them into the hands of plunderers, until he thrust them from his presence.* ***21*** *When he tore Israel away from the house of David, they made Jeroboam son of Nebat their king. Jeroboam enticed Israel away from following the LORD and caused them to commit a great sin.* ***22*** *The Israelites persisted in all the sins of Jeroboam and did not turn away from them* ***23*** *until the LORD removed them from his presence, as he had warned through all his servants the prophets. So the people of Israel were taken from their homeland into exile in Assyria, and they are still there.*

Tenacity of Idolatry of Judah (2 southern tribes) AFTER Solomon died UP TO the exile of the 2 southern tribes now called Judah

Rehoboam (king of Judah for 17 years)

> *1 Kings 14:22-24*
> **22** *Judah did evil in the eyes of the LORD. By the sins they committed they stirred up his jealous anger more than their fathers had done.* **23** *They also set up for themselves high places, sacred stones and Asherah poles on every high hill and under every spreading tree.* **24** *There were even male shrine prostitutes in the land; the people engaged in all the detestable practices of the nations the LORD had driven out before the Israelites.*

Abijah (king of Judah for 3 years)

> *1 Kings 15:3*
> **3** *He committed all the sins his father had done before him; his heart was not fully devoted to the LORD his God, as the heart of David his forefather had been.*

Asa (king of Judah for 41 years)

> *1 Kings 15:11-14*
> **11** *Asa did what was right in the eyes of the LORD, as his father David had done.* **12** *He expelled the male shrine prostitutes from the land and got rid of all the idols his fathers had made.* **13** *He even deposed his grandmother Maacah from her position as queen mother, because she had made a*

repulsive Asherah pole. Asa cut the pole down and burned it in the Kidron Valley. ***14*** *Although he did not remove the high places, Asa's heart was fully committed to the LORD all his life.*

2 Chronicles 14:3-5
3 *He removed the foreign altars and the high places, smashed the sacred stones and cut down the Asherah poles.* ***4*** *He commanded Judah to seek the LORD, the God of their fathers, and to obey his laws and commands.* ***5*** *He removed the high places and incense altars in every town in Judah, and the kingdom was at peace under him.*

2 Chronicles 15:8
8 *When Asa heard these words and the prophecy of Azariah son of Oded the prophet, he took courage. He removed the detestable idols from the whole land of Judah and Benjamin and from the towns he had captured in the hills of Ephraim. He repaired the altar of the LORD that was in front of the portico of the LORD's temple.*

2 Chronicles 15:16-17
16 *King Asa also deposed his grandmother Maacah from her position as queen mother, because she had made a repulsive Asherah pole. Asa cut the pole down, broke it up and burned it in the Kidron Valley.* ***17*** *Although he did not remove the high places from Israel, Asa's heart was fully committed [to the LORD] all his life.*

Jehoshaphat (king of Judah for 35 years)

1 Kings 22:43
43 *In everything he walked in the ways of his father Asa and did not stray from them; he did what was right in the eyes of the LORD. The high places, however, were not removed, and the people continued to offer sacrifices and burn incense there.*

2 Chronicles 20:32-33
32 *He walked in the ways of his father Asa and did not stray from them; he did what was right in the eyes of the LORD.* **33** *The high places, however, were not removed, and the people still had not set their hearts on the God of their fathers.*

2 Chronicles 17:6
6 *His heart was devoted to the ways of the LORD; furthermore, he removed the high places and the Asherah poles from Judah.*

1 Kings 22:46
46 *He rid the land of the rest of the male shrine prostitutes who remained there even after the reign of his father Asa.*

Jehoram (king of Judah for 8 years)

2 Kings 8:18
18 *He walked in the ways of the kings of Israel, as the house of Ahab had done, for he married a daughter of Ahab. He did evil in the eyes of the LORD.*

Ahaziah (king of Judah for 22 years)

2 Kings 8:26-27
26 *Ahaziah was twenty-two years old when he became king, and he reigned in Jerusalem one year. His mother's name was Athaliah, a granddaughter of Omri king of Israel.* ***27*** *He walked in the ways of the house of Ahab and did evil in the eyes of the LORD, as the house of Ahab had done, for he was related by marriage to Ahab's family.*

Athaliah (female ruler of Judah for 6 years while Joash was hidden as a child in the Temple)

2 Kings 11:17-18
[After Athaliah was put to death] ***17*** *Jehoiada [priest] then made a covenant between the LORD and the king and people that they would be the LORD's people. He also made a covenant between the king and the people.* ***18*** *All the people of the land went to the temple of Baal and tore it down. They smashed the altars and idols to pieces and killed Mattan the priest of Baal in front of the altars. Then Jehoiada the priest posted guards at the temple of the LORD.*

Joash (king of Judah for 40 years)

2 Kings 12:2-3
2 *Joash did what was right in the eyes of the LORD all the years Jehoiada the priest instructed him.*
3 *The high places, however, were not removed; the people continued to offer sacrifices and burn incense there.*

2 Chronicles 24:17-19
17 *After the death of Jehoiada, the officials of Judah came and paid homage to the king, and he listened to them.* ***18*** *They abandoned the temple of the LORD, the God of their fathers, and worshiped Asherah poles and idols. Because of their guilt, God's anger came upon Judah and Jerusalem.* ***19***
Although the LORD sent prophets to the people to bring them back to him, and though they testified against them, they would not listen.

Amaziah (king of Judah for 29 years)

2 Kings 14:3-4
3 *He did what was right in the eyes of the LORD, but not as his father David had done. In everything he followed the example of his father Joash.* ***4*** *The high places, however, were not removed; the people continued to offer sacrifices and burn incense there.*

Azariah (king of Judah for 52 years)

2 Kings 15:3-4
3 *He did what was right in the eyes of the LORD, just as his father Amaziah had done.* ***4*** *The high places, however, were not removed; the people continued to offer sacrifices and burn incense there.*

Isaiah prophesies against idolatry

Jotham (king of Judah for 16 years)

2 Kings 15:34-35
34 *He did what was right in the eyes of the LORD, just as his father Uzziah had done.* ***35*** *The high*

places, however, were not removed; the people continued to offer sacrifices and burn incense there. Jotham rebuilt the Upper Gate of the temple of the LORD.

Isaiah prophesies against idolatry.

Micah prophesies against idolatry.

Ahaz (king of Judah for 16 years)

2 Kings 16:2-4
***2** Ahaz was twenty years old when he became king,*
and he reigned in Jerusalem sixteen years. Unlike
David his father, he did not do what was right in
*the eyes of the LORD his God. **3** He walked in*
the ways of the kings of Israel and even sacrificed
his son in the fire, following the detestable ways
of the nations the LORD had driven out before
*the Israelites. **4** He offered sacrifices and burned*
incense at the high places, on the hilltops and
under every spreading tree.

2 Kings 16:10-16
***10** Then King Ahaz went to Damascus to meet*
Tiglath-Pileser king of Assyria. He saw an altar
in Damascus and sent to Uriah the priest a sketch
of the altar, with detailed plans for its construc-
*tion. **11** So Uriah the priest built an altar in*
accordance with all the plans that King Ahaz had
sent from Damascus and finished it before King
*Ahaz returned. **12** When the king came back from*
Damascus and saw the altar, he approached it
*and presented offerings on it. **13** He offered up his*
burnt offering and grain offering, poured out his

> *drink offering, and sprinkled the blood of his fellowship offerings on the altar.* ***14*** *The bronze altar that stood before the LORD he brought from the front of the temple--from between the new altar and the temple of the LORD--and put it on the north side of the new altar.* ***15*** *King Ahaz then gave these orders to Uriah the priest: "On the large new altar, offer the morning burnt offering and the evening grain offering, the king's burnt offering and his grain offering, and the burnt offering of all the people of the land, and their grain offering and their drink offering. Sprinkle on the altar all the blood of the burnt offerings and sacrifices. But I will use the bronze altar for seeking guidance."* ***16*** *And Uriah the priest did just as King Ahaz had ordered.*
>
> *2 Chronicles 28:24-25*
> ***24*** *Ahaz gathered together the furnishings from the temple of God and took them away. He shut the doors of the LORD's temple and set up altars at every street corner in Jerusalem.* ***25*** *In every town in Judah he built high places to burn sacrifices to other gods and provoked the LORD, the God of his fathers, to anger*

Isaiah prophesies against idolatry.

Micah prophesies against idolatry.

<u>Hezekiah (king of Judah for 29 years]</u>

[Six years into Hezekiah's reign in Judah, the nation of Israel was deported by Assyria.]

2 Kings 18:3-6
***3** He did what was right in the eyes of the LORD, just as his father David had done. **4** He removed the high places, smashed the sacred stones and cut down the Asherah poles. He broke into pieces the bronze snake Moses had made, for up to that time the Israelites had been burning incense to it. (It was called Nehushtan.) **5** Hezekiah trusted in the LORD, the God of Israel. There was no one like him among all the kings of Judah, either before him or after him. **6** He held fast to the LORD and did not cease to follow him; he kept the commands the LORD had given Moses.*

Isaiah prophesies against idolatry.

Micah prophesies against idolatry.

<u>Manasseh (king of Judah for 55 years)</u>

<u>2 Kings 21:2-9</u>
***2** He did evil in the eyes of the LORD, following the detestable practices of the nations the LORD had driven out before the Israelites. **3** He rebuilt the high places his father Hezekiah had destroyed; he also erected altars to Baal and made an Asherah pole, as Ahab king of Israel had done. He bowed down to all the starry hosts and worshiped them. **4** He built altars in the temple of the LORD, of which the LORD had said, "In Jerusalem I will put my Name." **5** In both courts of the temple of the LORD, he built altars to all the starry hosts. **6** He sacrificed his own son in the fire, practiced sorcery and divination, and consulted mediums and spiritists. He did much evil in the eyes of the LORD,*

provoking him to anger. ***7*** *He took the carved Asherah pole he had made and put it in the temple, of which the LORD had said to David and to his son Solomon, "In this temple and in Jerusalem, which I have chosen out of all the tribes of Israel, I will put my Name forever.* ***8*** *I will not again make the feet of the Israelites wander from the land I gave their forefathers, if only they will be careful to do everything I commanded them and will keep the whole Law that my servant Moses gave them."*
9 *But the people did not listen. Manasseh led them astray, so that they did more evil than the nations the LORD had destroyed before the Israelites.* ***10***
The LORD said through his servants the prophets:
11 *"Manasseh king of Judah has committed these detestable sins. He has done more evil than the Amorites who preceded him and has led Judah into sin with his idols.*

2 Chronicles 33:10-19
10 *The LORD spoke to Manasseh and his people, but they paid no attention.* ***11*** *So the LORD brought against them the army commanders of the king of Assyria, who took Manasseh prisoner, put a hook in his nose, bound him with bronze shackles and took him to Babylon.* ***12*** *In his distress he sought the favor of the LORD his God and humbled himself greatly before the God of his fathers.* ***13*** *And when he prayed to him, the LORD was moved by his entreaty and listened to his plea; so he brought him back to Jerusalem and to his kingdom. Then Manasseh knew that the LORD is God.* ***14*** *Afterward he rebuilt the outer wall of the City of David, west of the Gihon spring in the valley, as far as the entrance of the*

Fish Gate and encircling the hill of Ophel; he
also made it much higher. He stationed military
commanders in all the fortified cities in Judah. ***15***
He got rid of the foreign gods and removed the
image from the temple of the LORD, as well as
all the altars he had built on the temple hill and
in Jerusalem; and he threw them out of the city.
16 *Then he restored the altar of the LORD and*
sacrificed fellowship offerings and thank offerings
on it, and told Judah to serve the LORD, the God
of Israel. ***17*** *The people, however, continued to*
sacrifice at the high places, but only to the LORD
their God. ***18*** *The other events of Manasseh's*
reign, including his prayer to his God and the
words the seers spoke to him in the name of the
LORD, the God of Israel, are written in the annals
of the kings of Israel. ***19*** *His prayer and how God*
was moved by his entreaty, as well as all his sins
and unfaithfulness, and the sites where he built
high places and set up Asherah poles and idols
before he humbled himself--all are written in the
records of the seers.

Amon (king of Judah for 2 years)

2 Kings 21:21-22
20 *He did evil in the eyes of the LORD, as his*
father Manasseh had done. ***21*** *He walked in all*
the ways of his father; he worshiped the idols his
father had worshiped, and bowed down to them.
22 *He forsook the LORD, the God of his fathers,*
and did not walk in the way of the LORD.

Josiah (king of Judah for 31 years)

2 Kings 22:2
***2** He did what was right in the eyes of the LORD and walked in all the ways of his father David, not turning aside to the right or to the left.*

2 Kings 23:4-20
***4** The king ordered Hilkiah the high priest, the priests next in rank and the doorkeepers to remove from the temple of the LORD all the articles made for Baal and Asherah and all the starry hosts. He burned them outside Jerusalem in the fields of the Kidron Valley and took the ashes to Bethel. **5** He did away with the pagan priests appointed by the kings of Judah to burn incense on the high places of the towns of Judah and on those around Jerusalem--those who burned incense to Baal, to the sun and moon, to the constellations and to all the starry hosts. **6** He took the Asherah pole from the temple of the LORD to the Kidron Valley outside Jerusalem and burned it there. He ground it to powder and scattered the dust over the graves of the common people. **7** He also tore down the quarters of the male shrine prostitutes, which were in the temple of the LORD and where women did weaving for Asherah. **8** Josiah brought all the priests from the towns of Judah and desecrated the high places, from Geba to Beersheba, where the priests had burned incense. He broke down the shrines at the gates--at the entrance to the Gate of Joshua, the city governor, which is on the left of the city gate.*
9** Although the priests of the high places did not serve at the altar of the LORD in Jerusalem, they ate unleavened bread with their fellow priests. **10

He desecrated Topheth, which was in the Valley of Ben Hinnom, so no one could use it to sacrifice his son or daughter in the fire to Molech. ***11***
He removed from the entrance to the temple of the LORD the horses that the kings of Judah had dedicated to the sun. They were in the court near the room of an official named Nathan-Melech. Josiah then burned the chariots dedicated to the sun. ***12***
He pulled down the altars the kings of Judah had erected on the roof near the upper room of Ahaz, and the altars Manasseh had built in the two courts of the temple of the LORD. He removed them from there, smashed them to pieces and threw the rubble
into the Kidron Valley. ***13*** *The king also desecrated*
the high places that were east of Jerusalem on the south of the Hill of Corruption--the ones Solomon king of Israel had built for Ashtoreth the vile goddess of the Sidonians, for Chemosh the vile god of Moab, and for Molech the detestable god of the
people of Ammon. ***14*** *Josiah smashed the sacred*
stones and cut down the Asherah poles and cov-
ered the sites with human bones. ***15*** *Even the altar*
at Bethel, the high place made by Jeroboam son of Nebat, who had caused Israel to sin--even that altar and high place he demolished. He burned the high place and ground it to powder, and burned the
Asherah pole also. ***16*** *Then Josiah looked around,*
and when he saw the tombs that were there on the hillside, he had the bones removed from them and burned on the altar to defile it, in accordance with the word of the LORD proclaimed by the man of
God who foretold these things. ***17*** *The king asked,*
"What is that tombstone I see?" The men of the city said, "It marks the tomb of the man of God who came from Judah and pronounced against the

altar of Bethel the very things you have done to it."
***18** "Leave it alone," he said. "Don't let anyone*
disturb his bones." So they spared his bones and
those of the prophet who had come from Samaria.
***19** Just as he had done at Bethel, Josiah removed*
and defiled all the shrines at the high places that
the kings of Israel had built in the towns of Samaria
that had provoked the LORD to anger. ***20** Josiah*
slaughtered all the priests of those high places on
the altars and burned human bones on them. Then
he went back to Jerusalem.

2 Kings 23:24-25
***24** Furthermore, Josiah got rid of the mediums*
and spiritists, the household gods, the idols and
all the other detestable things seen in Judah and
Jerusalem. This he did to fulfill the requirements of
the law written in the book that Hilkiah the priest
had discovered in the temple of the LORD. ***25***
Neither before nor after Josiah was there a king
like him who turned to the LORD as he did--with
all his heart and with all his soul and with all his
strength, in accordance with all the Law of Moses.

The prophet Zephaniah speaks out against idolatry.

The prophet Jeremiah begins speaking out against idolatry, and continues to speak out through the deportation of Judah by Babylon.

<u>Jehoahaz (king of Judah for 3 months)</u>

<u>2 Kings 23:32</u>
***32** He did evil in the eyes of the LORD, just as his*
fathers had done.

The prophet Jeremiah speaks out against idolatry, and continues to speak out through the deportation of Judah by Babylon.

<u>Jehoiakim (king of Judah for 11 years)</u>

> *<u>2 Kings 23:37</u>*
> ***37** And he did evil in the eyes of the LORD, just as his fathers had done.*

The prophet Jeremiah speaks out against idolatry, and continues to speak out through the deportation of Judah by Babylon.

<u>Jehoiachin (king of Judah for 3 months)</u>

> *<u>2 Kings 24:9</u>*
> ***9** He did evil in the eyes of the LORD, just as his father had done.*

The prophet Jeremiah speaks out against idolatry, and continues to speak out through the deportation of Judah by Babylon.

<u>Zedekiah (last king of Judah before Judah is deported, 11 year reign)</u>

> *<u>2 Kings 24:19</u>*
> ***19** He did evil in the eyes of the LORD, just as Jehoiakim had done.*

> *2 Chronicles 36:14*
> ***14** Furthermore, all the leaders of the priests and the people became more and more unfaithful, following all the detestable practices of the nations and defiling the temple of the LORD, which he had consecrated in Jerusalem*

The prophet Habakkuk speaks against idolatry.

The prophet Jeremiah continues speaking out against idolatry through the deportation of Judah by Babylon.

Details on the reasons for Judah's deportation are given in *Jeremiah* and *Ezekiel*. Idolatry was the key reason.

TENACITY OF GREED

Greed has always existed as the normal state of the world. But the normal state of the world is not our focus in this book.

The tenacity of greed for the worldwide church of believers from the early church until today - over 2,000 years - is not revealed in Scripture - unless the book of *Revelation* and its visions apply to the church over that period and into today.

What little I know of church history would indicate greed has been very active in many, if not all, ages over the 2,000 years. From my personal observations in the U.S. and extensive business travel to 22 industrialized nations, I believe greed has been active in the churches in the U.S. and in the modern world over my lifetime. I have not traveled to the third world nations, but I have noticed that as the internet access in third world nations increases, the news of economic discontent increases. Is that happening for the churches there also? I don't know. But I believe the internet is a major influence towards greed.

I have been particularly interested in the history of the United States as it relates to greed. In my youth I was taught that the pilgrims came to the U.S. for religious freedom, and that the revolution against England was because of its oppression against the colonists.

What I did not know was the pilgrims persecuted those who did not agree with their religion, and killed Indians because they were regarded as heathens. The pilgrims also did not believe England had any business telling them what to do.

The colonists rebelled against England because of greed. The thirteen colonies were originally thirteen English "companies" and the slave labor in most of these companies was to keep the business costs down in order to be competitive in the world markets. The real driver to buy slaves and use them for labor was greed. Their dehumanization allowed the owners to avoid their guilt. The number of slaves compared to the total population was significant, particularly in the colonies that were based on farming (e.g., cotton, sugar).

The Boston Tea Party (part of the northern colonies) was also based on greed. England needed to dump cheap tea into the colonies at about 1/3rd the price of tea that was being imported by the colonists from other countries. England then added a tax (about 12%) on the very low priced tea being shipped to Boston. The impression I had as a youth, was this tax was exorbitant. But in fact the English tea including the tax allowed the Boston colonist to enjoy tea at much lower prices. The Boston cry of "no taxation without representation" was a political sham. The businessmen of Boston did not want to lose profits on the tea they had been importing from elsewhere.

I also learned how the U.S. government unlawfully took land from the native Indians for the interest of greed, took land from Mexico for the interest of greed, and threatened peaceful (at that time) Japan with military violence if they did not open their markets to United States trade.

I have also noticed that the world governments today are working to either return their countries to prosperity after the Great Recession, or, if third world countries, to enter the prosperity of the other nations. Those governments which do not succeed may be replaced by the populace which craves for more. The spirit of greed continues to be enormous across the world. The tenacity of greed through the world is understandable.

But that is the world. That is not the kingdom of the Son of God. What of those in the kingdom of the Son? They have followed the world in its greed. In some cases (prosperity gospel) they even preach greed, they preach idolatry.

The tenacity of greed through the church is a horror.

Why is idolatry (under the Old Covenant) and greed (under the New Covenant) so tenacious? Why is it so hard to get rid of? We will look at the influences in the next two chapters.

INFLUENCES TOWARDS IDOLATRY

Why is idolatry so tenacious?

First, there is the human condition that wants to worship something outside of himself or herself, that also wants to see if this can contribute to the safety he or she desires.

But there are also many influences to continue in idolatry.

Here we look at some of the groups that influenced idolatry under the Old Covenant.

- Their leaders
- The nations and peoples around them
- Their family members

THEIR LEADERS

Exodus 32:1-24
1 *When the people saw that Moses was so long in coming down from the mountain, they gathered around Aaron and said, "Come, make us gods who will go before us. As for this fellow Moses who brought us up out of Egypt, we don't know what*

*has happened to him." **2** **Aaron*** **[first high priest under the**
Old Covenant] *answered them, "Take off the gold earrings*
that your wives, your sons and your daughters are wearing, and
*bring them to me." **3** So all the people took off their earrings*
*and brought them to Aaron. **4** He took what they handed him*
and made it into an idol cast in the shape of a calf, fashioning it
with a tool. Then they said, "These are your gods, O Israel, who
*brought you up out of Egypt." **5** When Aaron saw this, he built*
an altar in front of the calf and announced, "Tomorrow there
*will be a festival to the LORD." **6** So the next day the people*
rose early and sacrificed burnt offerings and presented fellow-
ship offerings. Afterward they sat down to eat and drink and got
*up to indulge in revelry. **7** Then the LORD said to Moses, "Go*
down, because your people, whom you brought up out of Egypt,
*have become corrupt. **8** They have been quick to turn away from*
what I commanded them and have made themselves an idol cast
in the shape of a calf. They have bowed down to it and sacri-
ficed to it and have said, 'These are your gods, O Israel, who
*brought you up out of Egypt.' **9** "I have seen these people," the*
*LORD said to Moses, "and they are a stiff-necked people. **10***
Now leave me alone so that my anger may burn against them
and that I may destroy them. Then I will make you into a great
*nation." **11** But Moses sought the favor of the LORD his God.*
"O LORD," he said, "why should your anger burn against your
people, whom you brought out of Egypt with great power and
*a mighty hand? **12** Why should the Egyptians say, 'It was with*
evil intent that he brought them out, to kill them in the moun-
tains and to wipe them off the face of the earth'? Turn from your
*fierce anger; relent and do not bring disaster on your people. **13***
Remember your servants Abraham, Isaac and Israel, to whom
you swore by your own self: 'I will make your descendants as
numerous as the stars in the sky and I will give your descendants
all this land I promised them, and it will be their inheritance
*forever.' " **14** Then the LORD relented and did not bring on his*
*people the disaster he had threatened. **15** Moses turned and*

went down the mountain with the two tablets of the Testimony in his hands. They were inscribed on both sides, front and back. ***16*** *The tablets were the work of God; the writing was the writing of God, engraved on the tablets.* ***17*** *When Joshua heard the noise of the people shouting, he said to Moses, "There is the sound of war in the camp."* ***18*** *Moses replied: "It is not the sound of victory, it is not the sound of defeat; it is the sound of singing that I hear."* ***19*** *When Moses approached the camp and saw the calf and the dancing, his anger burned and he threw the tablets out of his hands, breaking them to pieces at the foot of the mountain.* ***20*** *And he took the calf they had made and burned it in the fire; then he ground it to powder, scattered it on the water and made the Israelites drink it.* ***21*** *He said to Aaron, "What did these people do to you, that you led them into such great sin?"* ***22*** *"Do not be angry, my lord," Aaron answered. "You know how prone these people are to evil.* ***23*** *They said to me, 'Make us gods who will go before us. As for this fellow Moses who brought us up out of Egypt, we don't know what has happened to him.'* ***24*** *So I told them, 'Whoever has any gold jewelry, take it off.' Then they gave me the gold, and I threw it into the fire, and out came this calf!"*

Joshua 24:1, 14-15
1 *Then Joshua assembled all the tribes of Israel at Shechem. He summoned the* ***elders, leaders, judges and officials of Israel****, and they presented themselves before God.*

14 *"Now fear the LORD and serve him with all faithfulness. Throw away the gods your forefathers worshiped beyond the River and in Egypt, and serve the LORD.* ***15*** *But if serving the LORD seems undesirable to you, then choose for yourselves this day whom you will serve, whether the gods your forefathers served beyond the River, or the gods of the Amorites, in whose land you are living. But as for me and my household, we will serve the LORD."*

Judges 8:23-27
23 *But* **Gideon [judge***] told them, "I will not rule over you, nor*
will my son rule over you. The LORD will rule over you." **24**
And he said, "I do have one request, that each of you give me
an earring from your share of the plunder." (It was the custom
of the Ishmaelites to wear gold earrings.) **25** *They answered,*
"We'll be glad to give them." So they spread out a garment,
and each man threw a ring from his plunder onto it. **26** *The*
weight of the gold rings he asked for came to seventeen hun-
dred shekels, not counting the ornaments, the pendants and the
purple garments worn by the kings of Midian or the chains that
were on their camels' necks. ***27 Gideon made the gold into an***
ephod, which he placed in Ophrah, his town. All Israel prosti-
tuted themselves by worshiping it there, and it became a snare
to Gideon and his family.

1 Kings 12:26-33
26 *Jeroboam thought to himself, "The kingdom will now likely*
revert to the house of David. **27** *If these people go up to offer*
sacrifices at the temple of the LORD in Jerusalem, they will
again give their allegiance to their lord, Rehoboam king of
Judah. They will kill me and return to King Rehoboam." **28**
After seeking advice, the king made two golden calves. He said
to the people, "It is too much for you to go up to Jerusalem.
Here are your gods, O Israel, who brought you up out of Egypt."
29 *One he set up in Bethel, and the other in Dan.* **30** *And this*
thing became a sin; the people went even as far as Dan to wor-
ship the one there. **31** *Jeroboam built shrines on high places and*
appointed priests *from all sorts of people, even though they were*
not Levites. **32** *He instituted a festival on the fifteenth day of the*
eighth month, like the festival held in Judah, and offered sacri-
fices on the altar. This he did in Bethel, sacrificing to the calves
he had made. And at Bethel he also ***installed priests at the high***
places *he had made.* **33** *On the fifteenth day of the eighth month,*
a month of his own choosing, he offered sacrifices on the altar he

had built at Bethel. So he instituted the festival for the Israelites and went up to the altar to make offerings.

1 Kings 13:33-34
***33** Even after this, Jeroboam did not change his evil ways, but once more appointed priests for the high places from all sorts of people. **Anyone who wanted to become a priest he consecrated for the high places. 34** This was the sin of the house of Jeroboam that led to its downfall and to its destruction from the face of the earth.*

Hosea 5:1-3
***1** "Hear this, **you priests**! Pay attention, you Israelites! Listen, O royal house! This judgment is against you: You have been a snare at Mizpah, a net spread out on Tabor. **2** The rebels are deep in slaughter. I will discipline all of them. **3** I know all about Ephraim; Israel is not hidden from me. Ephraim, **you have now turned to prostitution**; Israel is corrupt.*

Hosea 10:5
***5** The people who live in Samaria fear for the calf-idol of Beth Aven. Its people will mourn over it, and so will its **idolatrous priests**, those who had rejoiced over its splendor, because it is taken from them into exile.*

Hosea 4:9-12
9** And it will be: Like people, like **priests**. I will punish both of them for their ways and repay them for their deeds. **10** "They will eat but not have enough; they will engage in prostitution but not increase, because they have deserted the LORD to give themselves **11** to prostitution, to old wine and new, which take away the understanding **12** of my people. **They consult a wooden idol** and are answered by a stick of wood. **A spirit of prostitution leads them astray; they are unfaithful to their God.

Zephaniah 1:4
4 *"I will stretch out my hand against Judah and against all who live in Jerusalem. I will cut off from this place every remnant of Baal, the names of the pagan and* ***the idolatrous priests****—*

Isaiah 9:13-16
13 *But the people have not returned to him who struck them, nor have they sought the LORD Almighty.* ***14*** *So the LORD will cut off from Israel both head and tail, both palm branch and reed in a single day;* ***15 the elders*** *and prominent men are the head, the* ***prophets who teach lies*** *are the tail.* ***16 Those who guide this people mislead them, and those who are guided are led astray.***

Isaiah 30:8-11
8 *Go now, write it on a tablet for them, inscribe it on a scroll, that for the days to come it may be an everlasting witness.* ***9*** *These are rebellious people, deceitful children, children unwilling to listen to the LORD's instruction.* ***10*** *They say to the* ***seers****, "See no more visions!" and to the* ***prophets****, "Give us no more visions of what is right! Tell us pleasant things, prophesy illusions.* ***11***
Leave this way, get off this path, and stop confronting us with the Holy One of Israel!"

Jeremiah 2:8
8 The priests did not ask, 'Where is the LORD*?' Those who deal with the law did not know me; the leaders rebelled against me. The* ***prophets prophesied by Baal, following worthless idols****.*

Jeremiah 2:26-27
26 *"As a thief is disgraced when he is caught, so the house of Israel is disgraced-- they,* ***their kings and their officials, their priests and their prophets****.* ***27*** *They say to wood, 'You are my father,' and to stone, 'You gave me birth.' They have turned their backs to me and not their faces; yet when they are in trouble, they say, 'Come and save us!'*

Jeremiah 5:5

5 So I will go to the ***leaders*** *and speak to them; surely they know the way of the LORD, the requirements of their God." But with one accord they too had broken off the yoke and torn off the bonds.* ***6*** *Therefore a lion from the forest will attack them, a wolf from the desert will ravage them, a leopard will lie in wait near their towns to tear to pieces any who venture out, for their rebellion is great and their backslidings many.* ***7*** *"Why should I forgive you? Your children have forsaken me and sworn by gods that are not gods. I supplied all their needs, yet they committed adultery and thronged to the houses of prostitutes.* ***8*** *They are well-fed, lusty stallions, each neighing for another man's wife.* ***9*** *Should I not punish them for this?" declares the LORD. "Should I not avenge myself on such a nation as this?* ***10*** *"Go through her vineyards and ravage them, but do not destroy them completely. Strip off her branches, for these people do not belong to the LORD.* ***11*** *The house of Israel and the house of Judah have been utterly unfaithful to me," declares the LORD.* ***12*** *They have lied about the LORD; they said, "He will do nothing! No harm will come to us; we will never see sword or famine.* ***13*** *The* ***prophets*** *are but wind and the word is not in them; so let what they say be done to them."*

Jeremiah 5:30-31

30 *"A horrible and shocking thing has happened in the land:* ***31 The prophets prophesy lies****, the priests rule by their own authority, and my people love it this way. But what will you do in the end?*

Jeremiah 6:13-14

13 *"From the least to the greatest,* ***all are greedy for gain****;* ***prophets and priests*** *alike, all practice deceit.* ***14*** *They dress the wound of my people as though it were not serious. 'Peace, peace,' they say, when there is no peace.*

Jeremiah 14:13-16
***13** But I said, "Ah, Sovereign LORD, the prophets keep telling them, 'You will not see the sword or suffer famine. Indeed, I will give you lasting peace in this place.' " **14** Then the LORD said to me, "The **prophets** are prophesying lies in my name. I have not sent them or appointed them or spoken to them. They are prophesying to you false visions, divinations, idolatries and the delusions of their own minds. **15** Therefore, this is what the LORD says about the prophets who are prophesying in my name: I did not send them, yet they are saying, 'No sword or famine will touch this land.' Those same prophets will perish by sword and famine. **16** And the people they are prophesying to will be thrown out into the streets of Jerusalem because of the famine and sword. There will be no one to bury them or their wives, their sons or their daughters. I will pour out on them the calamity they deserve.*

Jeremiah 23:9-11
***9** " Concerning **the prophets**: My heart is broken within me; all my bones tremble. I am like a drunken man, like a man overcome by wine, because of the LORD and his holy words. **10** The land is full of adulterers; because of the curse the land lies parched and the pastures in the desert are withered. The [prophets] follow an evil course and use their power unjustly. **11** "Both prophet and priest are godless; even in my temple I find their wickedness," declares the LORD.*

Jeremiah 32:32-35
***32** The people of Israel and Judah have provoked me by all the evil they have done--they, **their kings and officials, their priests and prophets**, the men of Judah and the people of Jerusalem. **33** They turned their backs to me and not their faces; though I taught them again and again, they would not listen or respond to discipline. **34** They set up their abominable idols in the house that bears my Name and defiled it. **35** They built high places*

for Baal in the Valley of Ben Hinnom to sacrifice their sons and daughters to Molech, though I never commanded, nor did it enter my mind, that they should do such a detestable thing and so make Judah sin.

Lamentations 2:14
***14** The visions of your **prophets** were false and worthless; they did not expose your sin to ward off your captivity. The oracles they gave you were false and misleading*

Ezekiel 8:1-12
***1** In the sixth year, in the sixth month on the fifth day, while I was sitting in my house and **the elders of Judah** were sitting before me, the hand of the Sovereign LORD came upon me there.*
***2** I looked, and I saw a figure like that of a man. From what appeared to be his waist down he was like fire, and from there up his appearance was as bright as glowing metal. **3** He stretched out what looked like a hand and took me by the hair of my head. The Spirit lifted me up between earth and heaven and in visions of God he took me to Jerusalem, to the entrance to the north gate of the inner court, where the idol that provokes to jealousy stood. **4** And there before me was the glory of the God of Israel, as in the vision I had seen in the plain. **5** Then he said to me, "Son of man, look toward the north." So I looked, and in the entrance north of the gate of the altar I saw this idol of jealousy. **6** And he said to me, "Son of man, do you see what they are doing--the utterly detestable things the house of Israel is doing here, things that will drive me far from my sanctuary? But you will see things that are even more detestable." **7** Then he brought me to the entrance to the court. I looked, and I saw a hole in the wall. **8** He said to me, "Son of man, now dig into the wall." So I dug into the wall and saw a doorway there. **9** And he said to me, "Go in and see the wicked and detestable things they are doing here." **10** So I went in and looked, and I saw portrayed all over the walls all kinds of crawling things and detestable*

animals and all the idols of the house of Israel. ***11*** *In front of them stood* ***seventy elders of the house of Israel****, and Jaazaniah son of Shaphan was standing among them. Each had a censer in his hand, and a fragrant cloud of incense was rising.* ***12*** *He said to me, "Son of man, have you seen what the* ***elders of the house of Israel are doing in the darkness, each at the shrine of his own idol?*** *They say, 'The LORD does not see us; the LORD has forsaken the land.' "*

Ezekiel 13:1-16
1 *The word of the LORD came to me:* ***2*** *"Son of man, prophesy against the* ***prophets of Israel*** *who are now prophesying. Say to those who* ***prophesy out of their own imagination****: 'Hear the word of the LORD!* ***3*** *This is what the Sovereign LORD says: Woe to the foolish prophets who follow their own spirit and have seen nothing!* ***4*** *Your prophets, O Israel, are like jackals among ruins.* ***5*** *You have not gone up to the breaks in the wall to repair it for the house of Israel so that it will stand firm in the battle on the day of the LORD.* ***6 Their visions are false and their divinations a lie****. They say, "The LORD declares," when the LORD has not sent them; yet they expect their words to be fulfilled.* ***7*** *Have you not seen false visions and uttered lying divinations when you say, "The LORD declares," though I have not spoken?* ***8*** *" 'Therefore this is what the Sovereign LORD says: Because of your false words and lying visions, I am against you, declares the Sovereign LORD.* ***9*** *My hand will be against the prophets who see false visions and utter lying divinations. They will not belong to the council of my people or be listed in the records of the house of Israel, nor will they enter the land of Israel. Then you will know that I am the Sovereign LORD.* ***10*** *" 'Because they lead my people astray, saying,* ***"Peace," when there is no peace, and because, when a flimsy wall is built, they cover it with whitewash, 11*** *therefore tell those who cover it with whitewash that it is going to fall. Rain will come in torrents, and I will send hailstones hurtling down, and violent winds will burst forth.* ***12***

When the wall collapses, will people not ask you, "Where is the whitewash you covered it with?" ***13*** *" 'Therefore this is what the Sovereign LORD says: In my wrath I will unleash a violent wind, and in my anger hailstones and torrents of rain will fall with destructive fury.* ***14*** *I will tear down the wall you have covered with whitewash and will level it to the ground so that its foundation will be laid bare. When it falls, you will be destroyed in it; and you will know that I am the LORD.* ***15*** *So I will spend my wrath against the wall and against those who covered it with whitewash. I will say to you, "The wall is gone and so are those who whitewashed it,* ***16 those prophets of Israel who prophesied to Jerusalem and saw visions of peace for her when there was no peace****, declares the Sovereign LORD." '*

Ezekiel 14:1-5
1 *Some of the* ***elders of Israel*** *came to me and sat down in front of me.* ***2*** *Then the word of the LORD came to me:* ***3*** *"Son of man,* ***these men have set up idols in their hearts and put wicked stumbling blocks before their faces****. Should I let them inquire of me at all?* ***4*** *Therefore speak to them and tell them, 'This is what the Sovereign LORD says: When any Israelite sets up idols in his heart and puts a wicked stumbling block before his face and then goes to a prophet, I the LORD will answer him myself in keeping with his great idolatry.* ***5*** *I will do this to recapture the hearts of the people of Israel, who have all deserted me for their idols.'*

Ezekiel 22:25-28
25 *There is a conspiracy of her* ***princes*** *within her like a roaring lion tearing its prey; they devour people, take treasures and precious things and make many widows within her.* ***26*** *Her* ***priests*** *do violence to my law and profane my holy things; they do not distinguish between the holy and the common; they teach that there is no difference between the unclean and the clean; and they shut their eyes to the keeping of my Sabbaths, so that I am profaned among them.* ***27*** *Her* ***officials*** *within her are like wolves*

*tearing their prey; they shed blood and kill people to make unjust gain. **28** Her **prophets** whitewash these deeds for them by false visions and lying divinations. They say, 'This is what the Sovereign LORD says'--when the LORD has not spoken.*

Ezekiel 44:10-12
***10 " 'The Levites who went far from me when Israel went astray and who wandered from me after their idols must bear the consequences of their sin. 11** They may serve in my sanctuary, having charge of the gates of the temple and serving in it; they may slaughter the burnt offerings and sacrifices for the people and stand before the people and serve them. **12** But because they served them in the presence of their idols and made the house of Israel fall into sin, therefore I have sworn with uplifted hand that they must bear the consequences of their sin, declares the Sovereign LORD.*

THE NATIONS AND PEOPLES AROUND THEM

Numbers 25:1-3
***1** While Israel was staying in Shittim, the men began to indulge in sexual immorality **with Moabite women, 2 who invited them to the sacrifices to their gods**. The people ate and bowed down before these gods. **3** So Israel joined in worshiping the Baal of Peor. And the LORD's anger burned against them.*

Judges 3:1-6
***1** These are the **nations** the LORD left to test all those Israelites who had not experienced any of the wars in Canaan **2** (he did this only to teach warfare to the descendants of the Israelites who had not had previous battle experience): **3** the five rulers of the Philistines, all the Canaanites, the Sidonians, and the Hivites living in the Lebanon mountains from Mount Baal Hermon to Lebo Hamath. **4** They were left to test the Israelites to see whether they would obey the LORD's commands, which he*

had given their forefathers through Moses. ***5*** *The Israelites lived among the Canaanites, Hittites, Amorites, Perizzites, Hivites and Jebusites.* ***6 They took their daughters in marriage and gave their own daughters to their sons, and served their gods.***

1 Kings 16:30-33
30 *Ahab son of Omri did more evil in the eyes of the LORD than any of those before him.* ***31*** *He not only considered it trivial to commit the sins of Jeroboam son of Nebat, but he also* ***married Jezebel daughter of Ethbaal king of the Sidonians, and began to serve Baal and worship him.*** ***32*** *He set up an altar for Baal in the temple of Baal that he built in Samaria.* ***33*** *Ahab also made an Asherah pole and did more to provoke the LORD, the God of Israel, to anger than did all the kings of Israel before him.*

2 Kings 16:10-16
10 *Then King Ahaz went to Damascus to meet Tiglath-Pileser king of* **Assyria.** *He saw an altar in Damascus and sent to Uriah the priest a sketch of the altar, with detailed plans for its construction.* ***11*** *So Uriah the priest built an altar in accordance with all the plans that King Ahaz had sent from Damascus and finished it before King Ahaz returned.* ***12*** *When the king came back from Damascus and saw the altar, he approached it and presented offerings on it.* ***13*** *He offered up his burnt offering and grain offering, poured out his drink offering, and sprinkled the blood of his fellowship offerings on the altar.* ***14*** *The bronze altar that stood before the LORD he brought from the front of the temple--from between the new altar and the temple of the LORD--and put it on the north side of the new altar.* ***15*** *King Ahaz then gave these orders to Uriah the priest: "On the large new altar, offer the morning burnt offering and the evening grain offering, the king's burnt offering and his grain offering, and the burnt offering of all the people of the land, and their grain offering and their drink offering. Sprinkle on the altar all the blood of the burnt offerings and sacrifices. But I will use the bronze altar*

for seeking guidance." ***16*** *And Uriah the priest did just as King Ahaz had ordered.*

Psalms 106:34-39

34 *They did not destroy* **the peoples** *as the LORD had commanded them,* ***35*** *but they mingled with the nations and adopted their customs.* ***36*** *They worshiped their idols, which became a snare to them.* ***37*** *They sacrificed their sons and their daughters to demons.* ***38*** *They shed innocent blood, the blood of their sons and daughters, whom* ***they sacrificed to the idols of Canaan****, and the land was desecrated by their blood.* ***39*** *They defiled themselves by what they did; by their deeds they prostituted themselves.*

Ezekiel 16:14-29

[of Jerusalem] ***14*** *And* ***your fame spread among the nations*** *on account of your beauty, because the splendor I had given you made your beauty perfect, declares the Sovereign LORD.* ***15*** *" 'But you trusted in your beauty and* ***used your fame to become a prostitute****. You lavished your favors on anyone* **[nation]** *who passed by and your beauty became his.* ***16*** *You took some of your garments to make gaudy high places, where you carried on your prostitution. Such things should not happen, nor should they ever occur.* ***17*** *You also took the fine jewelry I gave you, the jewelry made of my gold and silver, and you made for yourself male idols and engaged in prostitution with them.* ***18*** *And you took your embroidered clothes to put on them, and you offered my oil and incense before them.* ***19*** *Also the food I provided for you--the fine flour, olive oil and honey I gave you to eat--you offered as fragrant incense before them. That is what happened, declares the Sovereign LORD.* ***20*** *" 'And you took your sons and daughters whom you bore to me and sacrificed them as food to the idols. Was your prostitution not enough?* ***21*** *You slaughtered my children and sacrificed them to the idols.* ***22*** *In all your detestable practices and your prostitution* *you did not remember the days of your youth, when you were naked and bare, kicking about in your blood.* ***23*** *" 'Woe! Woe to you, declares the Sovereign LORD. In addition to all your other wickedness,* ***24*** *you built a mound for yourself and made a lofty shrine in every public square.* ***25*** *At the head of every street you built your lofty shrines and degraded your beauty, offering your body with increasing promiscuity to anyone who passed by.* ***26*** *You engaged in prostitution with the* ***Egyptians****, your lustful neighbors, and provoked me to anger with your increasing promiscuity.* ***27*** *So I stretched out my hand against you and reduced your territory; I gave you over to the greed of your enemies, the daughters of the Philistines, who were shocked by your lewd conduct.* ***28*** *You engaged in prostitution with the* ***Assyrians*** *too, because you were insatiable; and even after that, you still were not satisfied.* ***29*** *Then you increased your promiscuity to include* ***Babylonia****, a land of merchants, but even with this you were not satisfied.*

Ezekiel 20:30-32
30 *"Therefore say to the house of Israel: 'This is what the Sovereign LORD says: Will you defile yourselves the way your fathers did and lust after their vile images?* ***31*** *When you offer your gifts--the sacrifice of your sons in the fire--you continue to defile yourselves with all your idols to this day. Am I to let you inquire of me, O house of Israel? As surely as I live, declares the Sovereign LORD, I will not let you inquire of me.* ***32*** *" 'You say, "****We want to be like the nations, like the peoples of the world, who serve wood and stone****." But what you have in mind will never happen.*

Ezekiel 23:1-21
1 *The word of the LORD came to me:* ***2*** *"Son of man, there were two women, daughters of the same mother.* ***3*** *They became prostitutes in* ***Egypt****, engaging in prostitution from their youth. In that land their breasts were fondled and their virgin bosoms*

caressed. **4** The older was named Oholah, and her sister was
Oholibah. They were mine and gave birth to sons and daughters.
Oholah is Samaria [capital of 10 northern tribes of Israel] and
Oholibah is Jerusalem [capital of 2 southern tribes of Israel]. **5**
"Oholah engaged in prostitution while she was still mine; and
she lusted after her lovers, the **Assyrians**--warriors **6** clothed in
blue, governors and commanders, all of them handsome young
men, and mounted horsemen. **7** She gave herself as a prostitute
to all the elite of the Assyrians and defiled herself with all the
idols of everyone she lusted after. **8** She did not give up the prostitution she began in Egypt, when during her youth men slept with
her, caressed her virgin bosom and poured out their lust upon
her. **9** "Therefore I handed her over to her lovers, the Assyrians,
for whom she lusted. **10** They stripped her naked, took away her
sons and daughters and killed her with the sword. She became a
byword among women, and punishment was inflicted on her. **11**
"Her sister Oholibah saw this, yet in her lust and prostitution
she was more depraved than her sister. 12 She too lusted after
the Assyrians--governors and commanders, warriors in full
dress, mounted horsemen, all handsome young men. **13** I saw
that she too defiled herself; both of them went the same way. **14**
"But she carried her prostitution still further. She saw men portrayed on a wall, figures of **Chaldeans** portrayed in red, **15** with
belts around their waists and flowing turbans on their heads;
all of them looked like **Babylonian** chariot officers, natives of
Chaldea. **16** As soon as she saw them, she lusted after them and
sent messengers to them in Chaldea. **17** Then the Babylonians
came to her, to the bed of love, and in their lust they defiled her.
After she had been defiled by them, she turned away from them
in disgust. **18** When she carried on her prostitution openly and
exposed her nakedness, I turned away from her in disgust, just
as I had turned away from her sister. **19** Yet she became more
and more promiscuous as she recalled the days of her youth,
when she was a prostitute in Egypt. **20** There she lusted after
her lovers, whose genitals were like those of donkeys and whose

emission was like that of horses. ***21*** *So you longed for the lewdness of your youth, when in Egypt your bosom was caressed and your young breasts fondled*

THEIR FAMILY MEMBERS

One of Jacob's two wives, Rachel, ***stole the household gods of her father*** *Laban who had descended from Nahor (Genesis 31:31-35), so Jacob's wife worshipped the idols of her father, a practice that may have come down from her ancestor -- great, great grandfather Terah who worshipped idols. The Israelites carried the idols of Terah's land with them into Egypt (Joshua 24:14).*

Deuteronomy 13:6-11
6 *If your very own* ***brother, or your son or daughter, or the wife you love, or your closest friend*** *secretly entices you, saying, "Let us go and worship other gods" (gods that neither you nor your fathers have known,* ***7*** *gods of the peoples around you, whether near or far, from one end of the land to the other),* ***8*** *do not yield to him or listen to him. Show him no pity. Do not spare him or shield him.* ***9*** *You must certainly put him to death. Your hand must be the first in putting him to death, and then the hands of all the people.* ***10*** *Stone him to death, because he tried to turn you away from the LORD your God, who brought you out of Egypt, out of the land of slavery.* ***11*** *Then all Israel will hear and be afraid, and no one among you will do such an evil thing again.*

Judges 17:1-6
1 *Now a man named Micah from the hill country of Ephraim*
2 *said to his mother, "The eleven hundred shekels of silver that were taken from you and about which I heard you utter a curse--I have that silver with me; I took it." Then his mother said, "The LORD bless you, my son!"* ***3*** *When he returned the eleven hundred shekels of silver to his mother,* ***she said, "I***

solemnly consecrate my silver to the LORD for my son to make a carved image and a cast idol. *I will give it back to you."* ***4*** *So he returned the silver to* ***his mother, and she took two hundred shekels of silver and gave them to a silversmith, who made them into the image and the idol.*** *And they were put in Micah's house.* ***5*** *Now this man Micah had a shrine, and he made an ephod and some idols and installed one of his sons as his priest.*

*1 Kings 15:*3 **[Note: this relationship of Judah's king to father or fathers is repeated many times.]**

3 *He committed all the sins* ***his father*** *had done before him; his heart was not fully devoted to the LORD his God, as the heart of David his forefather had been.*

1 Kings 15:9-13
9 *In the twentieth year of Jeroboam king of Israel, Asa became*
king of Judah, ***10*** *and he reigned in Jerusalem forty-one years.*
His grandmother's name was Maacah *daughter of Abishalom.*
11 *Asa did what was right in the eyes of the LORD, as his father*
David had done. ***12*** *He expelled the male shrine prostitutes from*
the land and got rid of all the idols his fathers had made. ***13***
He even deposed his grandmother Maacah from her position as queen mother, because she had made a repulsive Asherah pole*. Asa cut the pole down and burned it in the Kidron Valley.*

1 Kings 15:26 [Note: this relationship of Israel's king to father or fathers is repeated often.]

26 *He did evil in the eyes of the LORD, walking in the ways of his* ***father*** *and in his sin, which he had caused Israel to commit.*

1 Kings 16:30-33 [Baal worship enters Judah through Jezebel]

__30__ Ahab son of Omri did more evil in the eyes of the LORD than any of those before him. __31__ He not only considered it trivial to commit the sins of Jeroboam son of Nebat, but __he also married Jezebel daughter of Ethbaal king of the Sidonians, and began to serve Baal and worship him.__ __32__ He set up an altar for Baal in the temple of Baal that he built in Samaria. __33__ Ahab also made an Asherah pole and did more to provoke the LORD, the God of Israel, to anger than did all the kings of Israel before him.

1 Kings 18:4
__4__ While __Jezebel__ was killing off the LORD's prophets, Obadiah had taken a hundred prophets and hidden them in two caves, fifty in each, and had supplied them with food and water.)

1 Kings 19:1-3
__1__ Now Ahab told __Jezebel__ everything Elijah had done and how he had killed all the prophets with the sword. __2__ So __Jezebel__ sent a messenger to Elijah to say, "May the gods deal with me, be it ever so severely, if by this time tomorrow I do not make your life like that of one of them." __3__ Elijah was afraid and ran for his life.

1 Kings 21:25
__25__ (There was never a man like Ahab, who sold himself to do evil in the eyes of the LORD, urged on by __Jezebel his wife__.

2 Kings 8:16-18
__16__ In the fifth year of Joram son of Ahab king of Israel, when Jehoshaphat was king of Judah, Jehoram son of Jehoshaphat began his reign as king of Judah. __17__ He was thirty-two years old when he became king, and he reigned in Jerusalem eight years. __18 He walked in the ways of the kings of Israel, as the house of Ahab had done, for he married a daughter of Ahab__. He did evil in the eyes of the LORD.

2 Kings 8:25-27
***25** In the twelfth year of Joram son of Ahab king of Israel, Ahaziah son of Jehoram king of Judah began to reign. **26** Ahaziah was twenty-two years old when he became king, and he reigned in Jerusalem one year. **His mother's name was Athaliah, a granddaughter of Omri** king of Israel. **27** He walked in the ways of the house of Ahab and did evil in the eyes of the LORD, as the house of Ahab had done, for **he was related by marriage to Ahab's family**.*

2 Kings 11:1-2
***1** When Athaliah the **mother** of Ahaziah saw that her son was dead, she proceeded to destroy the whole royal family. **2** But Jehosheba, the daughter of King Jehoram and sister of Ahaziah, took Joash son of Ahaziah and stole him away from among the royal princes, who were about to be murdered. She put him and his nurse in a bedroom to hide him from Athaliah; so he was not killed. **3** He remained hidden with his nurse at the temple of the LORD for six years while Athaliah ruled the land. [She supported Baal worship in the land – 2 Kings 11:15-18]*

Isaiah 65:6-7
***6** "See, it stands written before me: I will not keep silent but will pay back in full; I will pay it back into their laps-- **7** both your sins and the sins of your **fathers**," says the LORD. "Because they burned sacrifices on the mountains and defied me on the hills, I will measure into their laps the full payment for their former deeds."*

Jeremiah 2:5
***5** This is what the LORD says: "What fault did your **fathers** find in me, that they strayed so far from me? They followed worthless idols and became worthless themselves.*

Jeremiah 3:22-25
22 *"Return, faithless people; I will cure you of backsliding." "Yes, we will come to you, for you are the LORD our God.* ***23*** *Surely the [idolatrous] commotion on the hills and mountains is a deception; surely in the LORD our God is the salvation of Israel.* ***24*** *From our youth shameful gods have consumed the fruits of our* ***fathers'*** *labor-- their flocks and herds, their sons and daughters.* ***25*** *Let us lie down in our shame, and let our disgrace cover us. We have sinned against the LORD our God, both we and* ***our fathers****; from our youth till this day we have not obeyed the LORD our God."*

Jeremiah 7:16-19
16 *"So do not pray for this people nor offer any plea or petition for them; do not plead with me, for I will not listen to you.* ***17*** *Do you not see what they are doing in the towns of Judah and in the streets of Jerusalem?* ***18 The children*** *gather wood,* ***the fathers*** *light the fire, and* ***the women*** *knead the dough and make cakes of bread for the Queen of Heaven. They pour out drink offerings to other gods to provoke me to anger.* ***19*** *But am I the one they are provoking? declares the LORD. Are they not rather harming themselves, to their own shame?*

Jeremiah 9:13-14
13 *The LORD said, "It is because they have forsaken my law, which I set before them; they have not obeyed me or followed my law.* ***14*** *Instead, they have followed the stubbornness of their hearts; they have followed the Baals,* ***as their fathers taught them****."*

Jeremiah 16:10-12, 19
10 *"When you tell these people all this and they ask you, 'Why has the LORD decreed such a great disaster against us? What wrong have we done? What sin have we committed against the LORD our God?'* ***11*** *then say to them, 'It is because* ***your fathers***

***forsook me**,' declares the LORD, 'and followed other gods and served and worshiped them. They forsook me and did not keep my law.* ***12** But **you have behaved more wickedly than your fathers**. See how each of you is following the stubbornness of his evil heart instead of obeying me.*

***19** O LORD, my strength and my fortress, my refuge in time of distress, to you the nations will come from the ends of the earth and say, "Our **fathers** possessed nothing but false gods, worthless idols that did them no good.*

Jeremiah 23:25-27
***25** "I have heard what the prophets say who prophesy lies in my name. They say, 'I had a dream! I had a dream!'* ***26** How long will this continue in the hearts of these lying prophets, who prophesy the delusions of their own minds?* ***27** They think the dreams they tell one another will make my people forget my name, just as their **fathers** forgot my name through Baal worship.*

Jeremiah 44:1, 7-10, 15-19, 24-26
***1** This word came to Jeremiah concerning all the Jews living in Lower Egypt--in Migdol, Tahpanhes and Memphis--and in Upper Egypt:*

***7** "Now this is what the LORD God Almighty, the God of Israel, says: Why bring such great disaster on yourselves by cutting off from Judah the men and women, the children and infants, and so leave yourselves without a remnant?* ***8** Why provoke me to anger with what your hands have made, burning incense to other gods in Egypt, where you have come to live? You will destroy yourselves and make yourselves an object of cursing and reproach among all the nations on earth.* ***9** Have you forgotten the wickedness committed by **your fathers** and by the kings and queens of Judah and the wickedness committed by you and **your wives** in the land of Judah and the streets of Jerusalem?* ***10** To this day they have not*

humbled themselves or shown reverence, nor have they followed
my law and the decrees I set before you and your fathers.

15 *Then all the men who knew that* ***their wives were burning***
incense to other gods*, along with all the women who were pres-*
ent--a large assembly--and all the people living in Lower and
Upper Egypt, said to Jeremiah, ***16*** *"We will not listen to the*
message you have spoken to us in the name of the LORD! ***17***
We will certainly do everything we said we would: We will burn
incense to the Queen of Heaven and will pour out drink offer-
ings to her just as we and our fathers, our kings and our offi-
cials did in the towns of Judah and in the streets of Jerusalem.
At that time we had plenty of food and were well off and suffered
no harm. ***18*** *But ever since we stopped burning incense to the*
Queen of Heaven and pouring out drink offerings to her, we have
had nothing and have been perishing by sword and famine." ***19***
The women added, "When we burned incense to the Queen
of Heaven and poured out drink offerings to her, did not our
husbands know that we were making cakes like her image and
pouring out drink offerings to her?"

24 *Then Jeremiah said to all the people,* ***including the women****,*
"Hear the word of the LORD, all you people of Judah in Egypt.
25 *This is what the LORD Almighty, the God of Israel, says: You*
and your wives have shown by your actions what you promised
when you said, 'We will certainly carry out the vows we made
to burn incense and pour out drink offerings to the Queen of
Heaven.' "Go ahead then, do what you promised! Keep your
vows! ***26*** *But hear the word of the LORD, all Jews living in*
Egypt: 'I swear by my great name,' says the LORD, 'that no
one from Judah living anywhere in Egypt will ever again invoke
my name or swear, "As surely as the Sovereign LORD lives."
27 *For I am watching over them for harm, not for good; the*
Jews in Egypt will perish by sword and famine until they are all
destroyed.

Ezekiel 13:17-23
17 *"Now, son of man, set your face against* **the daughters** *of your*
people who prophesy out of their own imagination. Prophesy
against them ***18*** *and say, 'This is what the Sovereign LORD says:*
Woe to the women who sew magic charms on all their wrists and
make veils of various lengths for their heads in order to ensnare
people. Will you ensnare the lives of my people but preserve
your own? ***19*** *You have profaned me among my people for a few*
handfuls of barley and scraps of bread. By lying to my people,
who listen to lies, you have killed those who should not have
died and have spared those who should not live. ***20*** *" 'Therefore*
this is what the Sovereign LORD says: I am against your magic
charms with which you ensnare people like birds and I will tear
them from your arms; I will set free the people that you ensnare
like birds. ***21*** *I will tear off your veils and save my people from*
your hands, and they will no longer fall prey to your power. Then
you will know that I am the LORD. ***22*** *Because you disheartened*
the righteous with your lies, when I had brought them no grief,
and because you encouraged the wicked not to turn from their
evil ways and so save their lives, ***23*** *therefore you will no longer*
see false visions or practice divination. I will save my people
from your hands. And then you will know that I am the LORD.' "

Ezekiel 20:23-24
23 *Also with uplifted hand I swore to them in the desert that I*
would disperse them among the nations and scatter them through
the countries, ***24*** *because they had not obeyed my laws but had*
rejected my decrees and desecrated my Sabbaths, and their eyes
[lusted] after their ***fathers' idols.***

Ezekiel 20:30
30 *"Therefore say to the house of Israel: This is what the*
Sovereign LORD says: Will you defile yourselves the way your
fathers *did and lust after their vile images?*

INFLUENCES TOWARDS GREED

Just as idolatry with Israel and Judah, there are influences towards greed for Christians. These influences can be by modeling (indirect) or by audio/visual (direct). Many of the following groups or similar groups are taken from the previous chapter, as they influenced God's people toward idolatry. I have added some additional groups that might support greed today.

You may want to think about the following groups and how some, or all, of these have been an influence on you towards greed.

SPIRITUAL LEADERS

Elders (overseers, bishops)

Pastors (or priests or apostles depending on the denomination)

Deacons

Preachers

Teachers

Book writers

Bloggers

Those with miraculous gifts (prophets, words of knowledge, healing)

WORLD

Government/laws

Nation histories and cultures (e.g., the American Dream)

Politicians

Financial institutions

Economists

News Media

Neighbors

Companies and institutes

Co workers

School

FAMILY

Culture

Husbands

Wives

Fathers

Mothers

Grandparents

In-laws

Sons

Daughters

BECOMING WORSE THAN THE OTHER NATIONS

There are some disturbing, and even puzzling, statements in the Old Testament about the comparison of Israel and Judah with each other, and with the other nations and even with Sodom.

First, some background. The Anakites were the "giants" that created fear in the Israelites so that they refused to enter the land after leaving Egypt. The Anakites were descendants (*Numbers 13:33)* from the Nephilim which were an unusual race (*"sons of God went to the daughters of men and had children by them")* at the time of the Flood (*Genesis 6:1-7)* and were part of the reason God decided to *"wipe mankind from the face of the earth"* by the Flood.

Because the Israelites had refused to enter the land after leaving Egypt, God had them wander in the desert for 40 years, at the end of which they again are faced with entering the land of Canaan. Before the Israelites crossed the Jordan River to take the land of Canaan, Moses by the Spirit reveals the following in *Deuteronomy 9:1-6.*

Deuteronomy 9:1-6
***1** Hear, O Israel. You are now about to cross the Jordan to go in and dispossess nations greater and stronger than you, with large cities that have walls up to the sky.* ***2** The people are strong and tall--Anakites! You know about them and have heard it said: "Who can stand up against the Anakites?"* ***3** But be assured today that the LORD your God is the one who goes across ahead of you like a devouring fire. He will destroy them; he will subdue them before you. And you will drive them out and annihilate them quickly, as the LORD has promised you.* ***4** After the LORD your God has driven them out before you, do not say to yourself, "The LORD has brought me here to take possession of this land because of my righteousness." No, it is on account of the wickedness of these nations that the LORD is going to drive them out before you.* ***5** It is not because of your righteousness or your integrity that you are going in to take possession of their land; but on account of the wickedness of these nations, the LORD your God will drive them out before you, to accomplish what he swore to your fathers, to Abraham, Isaac and Jacob.* ***6** Understand, then, that it is not because of your righteousness that the LORD your God is giving you this good land to possess, for you are a stiff-necked people.*

Deuteronomy 9:1-6 indicates that the LORD is going use the Israelites to drive the Anakites out of Canaan before them, but not because of the Israelites' righteousness, rather because of the wickedness of the Anakites and the other nations in Canaan. The land itself is important to God according to *Deuteronomy 11:11-12* – it is a land that God cares for, one that the eyes of the

LORD are continually on from the beginning of the year to its end. God wants to give this land that he cares for to the Israelites in spite of the fact that they are a stiff-necked people.

> *Deuteronomy 11:11-12*
> ***11** But the land you are crossing the Jordan to take possession of is a land of mountains and valleys that drinks rain from heaven. **12** It is a land the LORD your God cares for; the eyes of the LORD your God are continually on it from the beginning of the year to its end.*

The Israelites, a stiff-necked people waiting before entering the land, were to enter the land that God cared for and through observing the decrees and laws that God gave them would accomplish the following (*Deuteronomy* 4:5-8). They would show wisdom and understanding of God's righteous laws and decrees to the nations surrounding the land that God cared for, and this would reflect on God to the nations surrounding the land.

> *Deuteronomy 4:5-8*
> ***5** See, I have taught you decrees and laws as the LORD my God commanded me, so that you may follow them in the land you are entering to take possession of it. **6** Observe them carefully, for this will show your wisdom and understanding to the nations, who will hear about all these decrees and say, "Surely this great nation is a wise and understanding people." **7** What other nation is so great as to have their gods near them the way the LORD our God is near us whenever we pray to him? **8** And what other nation is so great as to have such righteous decrees and laws as this body of laws I am setting before you today?*

Now God gives a warning in *Deuteronomy 8:19-20* that if the Israelites forget God and follow other gods in the land God cares for, that God would destroy the Israelites just as He did the nations that were driven out of the land. In fact, God would scatter them out of the land he cared for into the surrounding nations (*Deuteronomy 4:25-28*).

> *Deuteronomy 8:19-20*
> ***19*** *If you ever forget the LORD your God and follow other gods and worship and bow down to them, I testify against you today that you will surely be destroyed.* ***20*** *Like the nations the LORD destroyed before you, so you will be destroyed for not obeying the LORD your God*
>
> *Deuteronomy 4:25-28*
> ***25*** *After you have had children and grandchildren and have lived in the land a long time--if you then become corrupt and make any kind of idol, doing evil in the eyes of the LORD your God and provoking him to anger,* ***26*** *I call heaven and earth as witnesses against you this day that you will quickly perish from the land that you are crossing the Jordan to possess. You will not live there long but will certainly be destroyed.* ***27*** *The LORD will scatter you among the peoples, and only a few of you will survive among the nations to which the LORD will drive you.* ***28*** *There you will worship man-made gods of wood and stone, which cannot see or hear or eat or smell.*

With the Israelites expelled from the land, then the land God cared for would have rest (*Leviticus* 26:32-35.

Leviticus 26:32-35
***32** I will lay waste the land, so that your ene-*
*mies who live there will be appalled. **33** I will*
scatter you among the nations and will draw out
my sword and pursue you. Your land will be laid
*waste, and your cities will lie in ruins. **34** Then*
the land will enjoy its sabbath years all the time
that it lies desolate and you are in the country of
your enemies; then the land will rest and enjoy its
*sabbaths. **35** All the time that it lies desolate, the*
land will have the rest it did not have during the
sabbaths you lived in it.

So, what happened?

In the period of the Judges (about 350 years), the Israelites went through cycles of idolatry and obedience, but the pattern in each cycle was to increase their corruptness compared to the previous cycle (*Judges* 2:19). So, a comparison of one cycle to another showed they were worse in each following cycle.

Judges 2:19
***19** But when the judge died, the people returned to ways even more corrupt than those of their fathers, following other gods and serving and worshiping them. They refused to give up their evil practices and stubborn ways.*

But during the period of the Judges God did not implement his warning to exude them from the land he cared for. Even after Solomon brought idolatry to Israel through the foreign wives he married, God divided the nation into the ten northern tribes (now called Israel) and the two southern tribes (now called Judah) but He still did not drive them out of the land.

After several hundred more years of idolatry, God finally drives Israel (10 northern tribes) out of the land and into Assyria. The charge was that (1) they followed the practices of the nations God had driven out before them, and (2) the practices that the kings of Israel had introduced. The latter practices were the two golden calves that King Jeroboam set up in Dan and Bethel *(1 Kings 12:28-30);* these were unique to Israel, and not from the practices of the nations that had been driven out. In this sense one might say that Israel exceeded the idolatry compared to the surrounding nations at that time because they followed the ways of the surrounding nations **plus** added their own special idolatry.

> *2 Kings 17:7-8*
> ***7** All this took place because the Israelites had sinned against the LORD their God, who had brought them up out of Egypt from under the power of Pharaoh king of Egypt. They worshiped other gods **8** and followed the practices of the nations the LORD had driven out before them, as well as the practices that the kings of Israel had introduced.*

What about Judah (2 southern tribes)?

They also did more evil than the nations that were originally driven out of the land.

> *2 Kings 21:1-9*
> ***1** Manasseh was twelve years old when he became king, and he reigned in Jerusalem fifty-five years. His mother's name was Hephzibah. **2** He did evil in the eyes of the LORD, following the detestable practices of the nations the LORD had driven out before the Israelites. **3** He rebuilt the high places his father Hezekiah had destroyed; he also erected*

altars to Baal and made an Asherah pole, as Ahab
king of Israel had done. He bowed down to all the
starry hosts and worshiped them. ***4*** *He built altars*
in the temple of the LORD, of which the LORD
had said, "In Jerusalem I will put my Name." ***5***
In both courts of the temple of the LORD, he built
altars to all the starry hosts. ***6*** *He sacrificed his*
own son in the fire, practiced sorcery and divi-
nation, and consulted mediums and spiritists. He
did much evil in the eyes of the LORD, provoking
him to anger. ***7*** *He took the carved Asherah pole*
he had made and put it in the temple, of which the
LORD had said to David and to his son Solomon,
"In this temple and in Jerusalem, which I have
chosen out of all the tribes of Israel, I will put
my Name forever. ***8*** *I will not again make the*
feet of the Israelites wander from the land I gave
their forefathers, if only they will be careful to do
everything I commanded them and will keep the
whole Law that my servant Moses gave them." ***9***
But the people did not listen. Manasseh led them
astray, so that **they did more evil than the nations**
the LORD had destroyed before the Israelites.

But, they changed their gods, something that no nation had ever done.

Jeremiah 2:11-12
11 *Has a nation ever changed its gods? (Yet they*
are not gods at all.) But my people have exchanged
their Glory for worthless idols. ***12*** *Be appalled at*
this, O heavens, and shudder with great horror,"
declares the LORD.

Judah looked at what God did to Israel and did not fear, but became widely unfaithful, and this even in the time of a good king (Josiah). God declared that faithless Israel (who had been already deported by the Assyrians) was more righteous than unfaithful Judah.

> *Jeremiah 3:6-11*
> ***6*** *During the reign of King Josiah, the LORD said to me, "Have you seen what faithless Israel has done? She has gone up on every high hill and under every spreading tree and has committed adultery there.* ***7*** *I thought that after she had done all this she would return to me but she did not, and her unfaithful sister Judah saw it.* ***8***
> *I gave faithless Israel her certificate of divorce and sent her away because of all her adulteries. Yet I saw that her unfaithful sister Judah had no fear; she also went out and committed adultery.*
> ***9*** *Because Israel's immorality mattered so little to her, she defiled the land and committed adultery with stone and wood.* ***10*** *In spite of all this, her unfaithful sister Judah did not return to me with all her heart, but only in pretense," declares the LORD.* ***11 The LORD said to me, "Faithless Israel is more righteous than unfaithful Judah.***

> *Ezekiel 5:5-7*
> ***5*** *"This is what the Sovereign LORD says: This is Jerusalem, which I have set in the center of the nations, with countries all around her.* ***6 Yet in her wickedness she has rebelled against my laws and decrees more than the nations and countries around her****. She has rejected my laws and has not followed my decrees.* ***7*** *"Therefore this is what the Sovereign LORD says: You have been*

> *more unruly than the nations around you and have not followed my decrees or kept my laws.* ***You have not even conformed to the standards of the nations around you.***

And what of Jerusalem, the city of David, the keeper of God's temple? God declared that Jerusalem exceeded the idolatry of Samaria, the capital of the Israel, by two times, and became more depraved than even Sodom.

Ezekiel 16:1-31, 42-52
1 *The word of the LORD came to me:* ***2*** *"Son of man, confront*
Jerusalem with her detestable practices ***3*** *and say, 'This is what*
the Sovereign LORD says to Jerusalem: Your ancestry and birth
were in the land of the Canaanites; your father was an Amorite
and your mother a Hittite. ***4*** *On the day you were born your cord*
was not cut, nor were you washed with water to make you clean,
nor were you rubbed with salt or wrapped in cloths. ***5*** *No one*
looked on you with pity or had compassion enough to do any of
these things for you. Rather, you were thrown out into the open
field, for on the day you were born you were despised. ***6*** *" 'Then*
I passed by and saw you kicking about in your blood, and as you
lay there in your blood I said to you, "Live!" ***7*** *I made you grow*
like a plant of the field. You grew up and developed and became
the most beautiful of jewels. Your breasts were formed and your
hair grew, you who were naked and bare.

8 *" 'Later I passed by, and when I looked at you and saw that you*
were old enough for love, I spread the corner of my garment over
you and covered your nakedness. I gave you my solemn oath and
entered into a covenant with you, declares the Sovereign LORD,
and you became mine. ***9*** *" 'I bathed you with water and washed*
the blood from you and put ointments on you. ***10*** *I clothed you*
with an embroidered dress and put leather sandals on you. I
dressed you in fine linen and covered you with costly garments.

11 I adorned you with jewelry: I put bracelets on your arms and a necklace around your neck, **12** and I put a ring on your nose, earrings on your ears and a beautiful crown on your head. **13** So you were adorned with gold and silver; your clothes were of fine linen and costly fabric and embroidered cloth. Your food was fine flour, honey and olive oil. You became very beautiful and rose to be a queen. **14** And your fame spread among the nations on account of your beauty, because the splendor I had given you made your beauty perfect, declares the Sovereign LORD.

15 " 'But you trusted in your beauty and used your fame to become a prostitute. You lavished your favors on anyone who passed by and your beauty became his. **16** You took some of your garments to make gaudy high places, where you carried on your prostitution. Such things should not happen, nor should they ever occur. **17** You also took the fine jewelry I gave you, the jewelry made of my gold and silver, and you made for yourself male idols and engaged in prostitution with them. **18** And you took your embroidered clothes to put on them, and you offered my oil and incense before them. **19** Also the food I provided for you--the fine flour, olive oil and honey I gave you to eat--you offered as fragrant incense before them. That is what happened, declares the Sovereign LORD. **20** " 'And you took your sons and daughters whom you bore to me and sacrificed them as food to the idols. Was your prostitution not enough? **21** You slaughtered my children and sacrificed them to the idols.

22 In all your detestable practices and your prostitution you did not remember the days of your youth, when you were naked and bare, kicking about in your blood. **23** " 'Woe! Woe to you, declares the Sovereign LORD. In addition to all your other wickedness, **24** you built a mound for yourself and made a lofty shrine in every public square. **25** At the head of every street you built your lofty shrines and degraded your beauty, offering your body with increasing promiscuity to anyone who passed by. **26**

You engaged in prostitution with the Egyptians, your lustful neighbors, and provoked me to anger with your increasing promiscuity. ***27*** *So I stretched out my hand against you and reduced your territory; I gave you over to the greed of your enemies, the daughters of the Philistines, who were shocked by your lewd conduct.* ***28*** *You engaged in prostitution with the Assyrians too, because you were insatiable; and even after that, you still were not satisfied.* ***29*** *Then you increased your promiscuity to include Babylonia, a land of merchants, but even with this you were not satisfied.* ***30*** *" 'How weak-willed you are, declares the Sovereign LORD, when you do all these things, acting like a brazen prostitute!* ***31*** *When you built your mounds at the head of every street and made your lofty shrines in every public square, you were unlike a prostitute, because you scorned payment.*

42 *Then my wrath against you will subside and my jealous anger will turn away from you; I will be calm and no longer angry.* ***43*** *" 'Because you did not remember the days of your youth but enraged me with all these things, I will surely bring down on your head what you have done, declares the Sovereign LORD. Did you not add lewdness to all your other detestable practices?* ***44*** *" 'Everyone who quotes proverbs will quote this proverb about you: "Like mother, like daughter."* ***45*** *You are a true daughter of your mother, who despised her husband and her children; and you are a true sister of your sisters, who despised their husbands and their children. Your mother was a Hittite and your father an Amorite.* ***46 Your older sister was Samaria, who lived to the north of you with her daughters; and your younger sister, who lived to the south of you with her daughters, was Sodom. 47 You not only walked in their ways and copied their detestable practices, but in all your ways you soon became more depraved than they. 48 As surely as I live, declares the Sovereign LORD, your sister Sodom and her daughters never did what you and your daughters have done. 49 " 'Now this was the sin of your sister Sodom: She and her daughters were***

arrogant, overfed and unconcerned; they did not help the poor and needy.* 50 *They were haughty and did detestable things before me. Therefore I did away with them as you have seen.* 51 *Samaria did not commit half the sins you did. You have done more detestable things than they, and have made your sisters seem righteous by all these things you have done.* 52 *Bear your disgrace, for you have furnished some justification for your sisters. Because your sins were more vile than theirs, they appear more righteous than you. So then, be ashamed and bear your disgrace, for you have made your sisters appear righteous.

One of the puzzles is how is it that God saw Judah as more unrighteous than Israel and Sodom? Judah had the Temple and God's priesthood, unlike Israel or Sodom. The reason, I believe, is that God measures righteousness not on an absolute scale, but based upon what He gives the people.

"From everyone who has been given much, much more will be demanded; and from the one who has been entrusted with much, much more will be asked." (Luke 12:47-48)

Judah was given the Temple and the priesthood, and Israel was not. Judah fell far shorter based upon what was given her compared to the fall of Israel who did not have the Temple and the priesthood of God. Likewise, Sodom had been given nothing.

Becoming worse than Sodom, Israel, and Judah

We saw at the end of the last chapter that God saw Judah, the one He had given the most to, as more unfaithful and unrighteous than Israel and Sodom. God requires more from those He gives more to. He had uniquely given Judah the Temple, where they could meet with God, and the Priesthood which could teach the people God's laws and decrees for their wisdom.

In the Old Testament God the Father declared Israel/Jerusalem was his Wife (*Hosea 2* and *Ezekie*l *16)*. In the New Testament we find that Jesus the Son of God is the head of the Church, in the same way that husbands are the head of their wives (*Ephesians 5:22-32)* and that the Lamb of God (Jesus) has a Bride, "those who hold to the testimony of Jesus (*Revelation 19:9-10)*.

The Wife of God the Father worshipped physical idols. Has the Bride of Christ likewise followed idolatry by way of greed?

God gave the Church a New Covenant in Christ's blood with the Holy Spirit to empower the Church to greater obedience. Through the Church God would teach his wisdom to the principalities and powers in the heavenly realms, according to His eternal purpose in Christ Jesus (*Ephesians 3:10-11)*.

Ephesians 3:10-11
10 *His [God's] intent was that now, through the church, the manifold wisdom of God should be made known to the rulers and authorities in the heavenly realms,* ***11*** *according to his eternal purpose which he accomplished in Christ Jesus our Lord.*

But has the Church pursued idolatry through greed for over two millennia?

Because God gave the Church more than He gave Israel and Judah, has the Church exceeded Sodom, Israel and Judah in unrighteousness? To whom much is given, much more is required.

Through the ages the Church has mocked Israel and Judah for their idols and called them apostate and then boasted of how much they (the Church) please God. Have they been like Judah when she looked at Israel's idolatry and punishment and had no fear?

Instead the Church, according to *Romans 11:13-32* should be afraid.

Romans 11:13-32
13 *I am talking to you Gentiles. Inasmuch as I am the apostle to*
the Gentiles, I make much of my ministry ***14*** *in the hope that I*
may somehow arouse my own people [Israelites] *to envy and save*
some of them. ***15*** *For if their rejection is the reconciliation of the*
world, what will their acceptance be but life from the dead? ***16*** *If*
the part of the dough offered as firstfruits is holy, then the whole
batch is holy; if the root is holy, so are the branches [Israel and
the Church]. ***17*** *If some of the branches* [Israel] *have been broken*
off, and you [the Church], *though a wild olive shoot, have been*
grafted in among the others and now share in the nourishing sap
from the olive root, ***18 do not boast over those branches. If you***

do, consider this: You do not support the root, but the root sup-
ports you. 19 You will say then, "Branches [Israel] ***were broken***
off so that I could be grafted in." 20 Granted. But they were
broken off because of unbelief, and you stand by faith. Do not
be arrogant, but be afraid. 21 For if God did not spare the nat-
ural branches [Israel], ***he will not spare you*** [the Church] ***either.***
22 Consider therefore the kindness and sternness of God: stern-
ness to those who fell, but kindness to you, provided that you
continue in his kindness. Otherwise, you also will be cut off. 23
And if they do not persist in unbelief, they will be grafted in, for
God is able to graft them in again. ***24*** *After all, if you were cut out*
of an olive tree that is wild by nature, and contrary to nature were
grafted into a cultivated olive tree, how much more readily will
these, the natural branches, be grafted into their own olive tree!

25 *I do not want you to be ignorant of this mystery, brothers, so*
that you **may not be conceited**: *Israel has experienced a hard-*
ening in part until the full number of the Gentiles has come in.
26 *And so all Israel will be saved, as it is written: "The deliverer*
will come from Zion; he will turn godlessness away from Jacob.
27 *And this is my covenant with them when I take away their*
sins." ***28*** *As far as the gospel is concerned, they are enemies on*
your account; but as far as election is concerned, they are loved
on account of the patriarchs, ***29*** *for God's gifts and his call are*
irrevocable. ***30*** *Just as you who were at one time disobedient to*
God have now received mercy as a result of their disobedience,
31 *so they too have now become disobedient in order that they*
too may now receive mercy as a result of God's mercy to you. ***32***
For God has bound all men over to disobedience so that he may
have mercy on them all.

GOD'S RESPONSES TO IDOLATRY

We will look at God's response to his people entering idolatry in three sections: God's feelings, God's warnings, and God's judgments.

HIS FEELINGS

His Jealousy

When God first gave the ten commandments of the Old Covenant, he told the people that he was a **jealous God** when it came to their bowing down and worshipping idols (*Exodus 20:4-6*). This revelation, which is part of the covenant agreement, is key to understanding God's warnings and judgments to the idolatry of his people. His jealously for his people is a feeling. These people are His, His Wife in fact. He knows the best for his people is to be faithful to Him alone. He knows the destruction that idolatry brings to His people (we saw this in chapter 5, "What happens to those who have idols?"). He is jealous for their sake. (We will also find this under the New Covenant – *James 4:4-6; 1 Corinthians 10:21-22.)*

> *Exodus 20:4-6*
> ***4*** *"You shall not make for yourself an idol in the form of anything in heaven above or on the earth beneath or in the waters below.* **5 You shall not bow down to them or worship them; for I, the LORD your God, am a jealous God**, *punishing the children for the sin of the fathers to the third and fourth generation of those who hate me,* ***6*** *but showing love to a thousand generations] of those who love me and keep my commandments.*

God's name is Jealous.

> *Exodus 34:10-16*
> ***10*** *Then the LORD said: "I am making a covenant with you. Before all your people I will do wonders never before done in any nation in all the world. The people you live among will see how awesome is the work that I, the LORD, will do for you.* ***11*** *Obey what I command you today. I will drive out before you the Amorites, Canaanites, Hittites, Perizzites, Hivites and Jebusites.* ***12*** *Be careful not to make a treaty with those who live in the land where you are going, or they will be a snare among you.* ***13*** *Break down their altars, smash their sacred stones and cut down their Asherah poles.* ***14*** *Do not worship any other god, for* **the LORD, whose name is *Jealous***, *is a jealous God.* ***15*** *"Be careful not to make a treaty with those who live in the land; for when they prostitute themselves to their gods and sacrifice to them, they will invite you and you will eat their sacrifices.* ***16*** *And when you choose some of their daughters as wives for your sons and those daughters prostitute themselves to their gods, they will lead your sons to do the same.*

God reiterates his jealousy 40 years after leaving Mount Sinai, just before the Israelites enter Canaan. (*Deuteronomy 4:23-24; 6:14-15*)

> *Deuteronomy 4:23-24*
> ***23** Be careful not to forget the covenant of the LORD your God that he made with you; do not make for yourselves an idol in the form of anything the LORD your God has forbidden.* ***24*** *For the LORD your* ***God is a consuming fire, a jealous God.***
>
> *Deuteronomy 6:14-15*
> ***14*** *Do not follow other gods, the gods of the peoples around you;* ***15*** *for the LORD your God, who is among you, is* ***a jealous God*** *and his anger will burn against you, and he will destroy you from the face of the land.*

<u>His Anger</u>

God's jealousy and anger go together when it comes to idols. His jealousy (you are MINE) leads to his anger over what is happening.

> *Deuteronomy 4:24*
> *For the LORD your God is* ***a consuming fire****, a jealous God.*
>
> *Deuteronomy 6:15*
> *for the LORD your God, who is among you, is a* ***jealous*** *God and* ***his anger*** *will burn against you, and he will destroy you from the face of the land.*

Deuteronomy 32:16
*They made him **jealous** with their foreign gods and **angered** him with their detestable idols.*

Deuteronomy 32:21
*They made me **jealous** by what is no god and **angered** me with their worthless idols. I will make them envious by those who are not a people; I will make them angry by a nation that has no understanding*

1 Kings 14:22
*Judah did evil in the eyes of the LORD. By the sins they committed they stirred up his **jealous anger** more than their fathers had done.*

Psalm 78:58
*They **angered him** with their high places; they aroused his **jealousy** with their idols.*

Psalm 79:5
*How long, O LORD? Will you be **angry** forever? How long will your **jealous**y burn like fire?*

Ezekiel 8:1-18
***1** In the sixth year, in the sixth month on the fifth day, while I was sitting in my house and the elders of Judah were sitting before me, the hand of the Sovereign LORD came upon me there. **2** I looked, and I saw a figure like that of a man. From what appeared to be his waist down he was like fire, and from there up his appearance was as bright as glowing metal. **3** He stretched out what looked like a hand and took me by the hair of my head. The Spirit lifted me up between earth and heaven*

and in visions of God he took me to Jerusalem, to
the entrance to the north gate of the inner court,
where **the idol that provokes to jealousy** stood. **4**
And there before me was the glory of the God of
Israel, as in the vision I had seen in the plain. **5**
Then he said to me, "Son of man, look toward the
north." So I looked, and in the entrance north of
the gate of the altar I saw this **idol of jealousy**. **6**
And he said to me, "Son of man, do you see what
they are doing--the utterly detestable things the
house of Israel is doing here, things that will drive
me far from my sanctuary? But you will see things
that are even more detestable." **7** Then he brought
me to the entrance to the court. I looked, and I
saw a hole in the wall. **8** He said to me, "Son of
man, now dig into the wall." So I dug into the wall
and saw a doorway there. **9** And he said to me,
"Go in and see the wicked and detestable things
they are doing here." **10** So I went in and looked,
and I saw portrayed all over the walls all kinds
of crawling things and detestable animals and all
the idols of the house of Israel. **11** In front of them
stood seventy elders of the house of Israel, and
Jaazaniah son of Shaphan was standing among
them. Each had a censer in his hand, and a fragrant cloud of incense was rising. **12** He said to
me, "Son of man, have you seen what the elders
of the house of Israel are doing in the darkness,
each at the shrine of his own idol? They say, 'The
LORD does not see us; the LORD has forsaken
the land.' " **13** Again, he said, "You will see them
doing things that are even more detestable." **14**
Then he brought me to the entrance to the north
gate of the house of the LORD, and I saw women
sitting there, mourning for Tammuz. **15** He said

to me, "Do you see this, son of man? You will see things that are even more detestable than this." ***16*** *He then brought me into the inner court of the house of the LORD, and there at the entrance to the temple, between the portico and the altar, were about twenty-five men. With their backs toward the temple of the LORD and their faces toward the east, they were bowing down to the sun in the east.* ***17*** *He said to me, "Have you seen this, son of man? Is it a trivial matter for the house of Judah to do the detestable things they are doing here? Must they also fill the land with violence and* ***continually provoke me to anger****? Look at them putting the branch to their nose!* ***18 Therefore I will deal with them in anger****; I will not look on them with pity or spare them. Although they shout in my ears, I will not listen to them."*

Ezekiel 16:38
I will sentence you to the punishment of women who commit adultery and who shed blood; I will bring upon you the blood vengeance of my wrath ***jealous anger****.*

Ezekiel 16:42
Then my wrath against you will subside and my ***jealous anger*** *will turn away from you; I will be calm and no longer angry*

His Grieving

So, God has jealousy and anger when His people, who are His, follow after idols, bow down to them and worship them. But God also grieves.

Ezekiel 6:9-10
9 *Then in the nations where they have been carried captive, those who escape will remember me--how* ***I have been grieved by their adulterous hearts, which have turned away from me, and by their eyes, which have lusted after their idols****. They will loathe themselves for the evil they have done and for all their detestable practices.* ***10*** *And they will know that I am the LORD; I did not threaten in vain to bring this calamity on them.*

HIS WARNINGS

Because God knew the damage that idolatry would bring to his people, God warned them. God repeatedly warned his people through his prophets. The prophets confronted the people primarily with their idolatry, but also with their oppression. (Where there is idolatry, there is oppression.) By turning the people from their evil ways and deeds, and by implication back to loving God and their neighbor, the prophets' words hang on the two great commandments.

Jeremiah 23:22
22 *But if they [prophets] had stood in my council, they would have proclaimed my words to my people and would have turned them from their evil ways and from their evil deeds.*

The main prophets and their warnings for Israel and Judah up to their deportation from the land came from:

Moses (*Deuteronomy*)

Elijah and Elisha (*1&2 Kings*)

Hosea (*Hosea*)

Amos (*Amos*)

Isaiah (*Isaiah*)

Jeremiah (*Jeremiah*)

Ezekiel (*Ezekiel*)

HIS JUDGMENTS

After repeated warnings over a very long time, God took action to separate his people from their idolatry which was destroying them. One of the puzzles is that God used ungodly nations (e.g. Aram, Moab, Canaan, Midian, Philistia, and Ammon in the period of the Judges; Assyria for Israel; and Babylon for Judah) to bring these judgments. This puzzle was particularly troubling for the prophet Habakkuk.

Judgment of idols and gods

> *Hosea 10:5-6*
> *5 The people who live in Samaria* ***fear for the calf-idol of Beth Aven****. Its people will mourn over it, and so will its idolatrous priests, those who had rejoiced over its splendor, because it is taken from them into exile.* ***6 It will be carried to Assyria as tribute for the great king****. Ephraim will be disgraced; Israel will be ashamed of its wooden idols*
>
> *Jeremiah 10:11-16*
> ***11*** *"Tell them this:* ***'These gods****, who did not make the heavens and the earth,* ***will perish*** *from the earth and from under the heavens.' "* ***12*** *But*

God made the earth by his power; he founded the world by his wisdom and stretched out the heavens by his understanding. ***13*** *When he thunders, the waters in the heavens roar; he makes clouds rise from the earth. He sends lightning with the rain and brings out the wind from his storehouses.* ***14*** *Everyone is senseless and without knowledge; every goldsmith is shamed by his idols.* ***His images*** *are a fraud; they have no breath in them.* ***15*** *They are worthless, the objects of mockery;* ***when their judgment comes, they will perish.*** ***16*** *He who is the Portion of Jacob is not like these, for he is the Maker of all things, including Israel, the tribe of his inheritance-- the LORD Almighty is his name.*

<u>Judgment of the idolaters</u>

Of Israel (12 tribes together)

Before entering the land of Canaan

Numbers 25:1-9
1 *While Israel was staying in Shittim, the men began to indulge in sexual immorality with Moabite women,* ***2*** *who invited them to the sacrifices to their gods. The people ate and bowed down before these gods.* ***3*** *So Israel joined in worshiping the Baal of Peor. And the LORD's anger burned against them.* ***4*** *The LORD said to Moses, "Take all the leaders of these people, kill them and expose them in broad daylight before the LORD, so that the LORD's fierce anger may turn away from Israel."* ***5*** *So Moses said to Israel's judges, "Each of you must put to death those of your men*

who have joined in worshiping the Baal of Peor."
6 *Then an Israelite man brought to his family a*
Midianite woman right before the eyes of Moses
and the whole assembly of Israel while they were
weeping at the entrance to the Tent of Meeting. ***7***
When Phinehas son of Eleazar, the son of Aaron,
the priest, saw this, he left the assembly, took a
spear in his hand ***8*** *and followed the Israelite*
into the tent. He drove the spear through both of
them--through the Israelite and into the woman's
body. Then the plague against the Israelites was
stopped; ***9*** *but those who died in the plague num-*
bered 24,000.

<u>During the period of the judges</u>

<u>*Judges 2:10-23*</u>
10 *After that whole generation had been gathered to their*
fathers, another generation grew up, who knew neither the
LORD nor what he had done for Israel. ***11*** *Then the Israelites*
did evil in the eyes of the LORD and served the Baals. ***12*** *They*
forsook the LORD, the God of their fathers, who had brought
them out of Egypt. They followed and worshiped various gods of
the peoples around them. They provoked the LORD to anger ***13***
because they forsook him and served Baal and the Ashtoreths.
14 *In his anger against Israel the LORD handed them over to*
raiders who plundered them. He sold them to their enemies all
around, whom they were no longer able to resist. ***15*** *Whenever*
Israel went out to fight, the hand of the LORD was against them
to defeat them, just as he had sworn to them. They were in great
distress. ***16*** *Then the LORD raised up judges, who saved them*
out of the hands of these raiders. ***17*** *Yet they would not listen to*
their judges but prostituted themselves to other gods and wor-
shiped them. Unlike their fathers, they quickly turned from the
way in which their fathers had walked, the way of obedience

to the LORD's commands. ***18*** *Whenever the LORD raised up a judge for them, he was with the judge and saved them out of the hands of their enemies as long as the judge lived; for the LORD had compassion on them as they groaned under those who oppressed and afflicted them.* ***19*** *But when the judge died, the people returned to ways even more corrupt than those of their fathers, following other gods and serving and worshiping them. They refused to give up their evil practices and stubborn ways.* ***20*** *Therefore the LORD was very angry with Israel and said, "Because this nation has violated the covenant that I laid down for their forefathers and has not listened to me,* ***21*** *I will no longer drive out before them any of the nations Joshua left when he died.* ***22*** *I will use them to test Israel and see whether they will keep the way of the LORD and walk in it as their forefathers did."* ***23*** *The LORD had allowed those nations to remain; he did not drive them out at once by giving them into the hands of Joshua.*

<u>For Israel, the 10 northern tribes</u>

<u>Hosea 2:5-13</u>
5 *Their mother has been unfaithful and has conceived them in disgrace. She said, 'I will go after my lovers, who give me my food and my water, my wool and my linen, my oil and my drink.'*
6 *Therefore I will block her path with thornbushes; I will wall her in so that she cannot find her way.* ***7*** *She will chase after her lovers but not catch them; she will look for them but not find them. Then she will say, 'I will go back to my husband as at first, for then I was better off than now.'* ***8*** *She has not acknowledged that I was the one who gave her the grain, the new wine and oil, who lavished on her the silver and gold-- which they used for Baal.* ***9*** *"Therefore I will take away my grain when it ripens, and my new wine when it is ready. I will take back my wool and my linen, intended to cover her nakedness.* ***10*** *So now I will expose her lewdness before the eyes of her lovers; no one will take her*

out of my hands. ***11*** *I will stop all her celebrations: her yearly*
festivals, her New Moons, her Sabbath days--all her appointed
feasts. ***12*** *I will ruin her vines and her fig trees, which she said*
were her pay from her lovers; I will make them a thicket, and
wild animals will devour them. ***13*** *I will punish her for the days*
she burned incense to the Baals; she decked herself with rings
and jewelry, and went after her lovers, but me she forgot,"
declares the LORD.

Hosea 9:1-4
1 *Do not rejoice, O Israel; do not be jubilant like the other*
nations. For you have been unfaithful to your God; you love the
wages of a prostitute at every threshing floor. ***2*** *Threshing floors*
and winepresses will not feed the people; the new wine will fail
them. ***3*** *They will not remain in the LORD's land; Ephraim will*
return to Egypt and eat unclean food in Assyria. ***4*** *They will*
not pour out wine offerings to the LORD, nor will their sacri-
fices please him. Such sacrifices will be to them like the bread of
mourners; all who eat them will be unclean. This food will be for
themselves; it will not come into the temple of the LORD.

Amos 4:1-12
1 *Hear this word, you cows of Bashan on Mount Samaria, you*
women who oppress the poor and crush the needy and say to
your husbands, "Bring us some drinks!" ***2*** *The Sovereign LORD*
has sworn by his holiness: "The time will surely come when you
will be taken away with hooks, the last of you with fishhooks.
3 *You will each go straight out through breaks in the wall, and*
you will be cast out toward Harmon, " declares the LORD. ***4***
"Go to Bethel and sin; go to Gilgal and sin yet more. Bring your
sacrifices every morning, your tithes every three years. ***5*** *Burn*
leavened bread as a thank offering and brag about your free-
will offerings-- boast about them, you Israelites, for this is what
you love to do," declares the Sovereign LORD. ***6*** *"I gave you*
empty stomachs in every city and lack of bread in every town,

yet you have not returned to me," declares the LORD. ***7*** *"I also withheld rain from you when the harvest was still three months away. I sent rain on one town, but withheld it from another. One field had rain; another had none and dried up.* ***8*** *People staggered from town to town for water but did not get enough to drink, yet you have not returned to me," declares the LORD.* ***9***
"Many times I struck your gardens and vineyards, I struck them with blight and mildew. Locusts devoured your fig and olive trees, yet you have not returned to me," declares the LORD.
10 *"I sent plagues among you as I did to Egypt. I killed your young men with the sword, along with your captured horses. I filled your nostrils with the stench of your camps, yet you have not returned to me," declares the LORD.* ***11*** *"I overthrew some of you as I overthrew Sodom and Gomorrah. You were like a burning stick snatched from the fire, yet you have not returned to me," declares the LORD.* ***12*** *"Therefore this is what I will do to you, Israel, and because I will do this to you, prepare to meet your God, O Israel."*

Isaiah 10:5
5 *"Woe to the Assyrian, the rod of my anger, in whose hand is the club of my wrath!*

2 Kings 15:17-20
17 *In the thirty-ninth year of Azariah king of Judah, Menahem son of Gadi became king of Israel, and he reigned in Samaria ten years.* ***18*** *He did evil in the eyes of the LORD. During his entire reign he did not turn away from the sins of Jeroboam son of Nebat, which he had caused Israel to commit.* ***19*** *Then Pul king of Assyria invaded the land, and Menahem gave him a thousand talents of silver to gain his support and strengthen his own hold on the kingdom.* ***20*** *Menahem exacted this money from Israel. Every wealthy man had to contribute fifty shekels of silver to be given to the king of Assyria. So the king of Assyria withdrew and stayed in the land no longer.*

2 Kings 15:27-29

27 *In the fifty-second year of Azariah king of Judah, Pekah son of Remaliah became king of Israel in Samaria, and he reigned twenty years.* **28** *He did evil in the eyes of the LORD. He did not turn away from the sins of Jeroboam son of Nebat, which he had caused Israel to commit.* **29** *In the time of Pekah king of Israel, Tiglath-Pileser king of Assyria came and took Ijon, Abel Beth Maacah, Janoah, Kedesh and Hazor. He took Gilead and Galilee, including all the land of Naphtali, and deported the people to Assyria.*

2 Kings 16:1-9

1 *In the seventeenth year of Pekah son of Remaliah, Ahaz son of Jotham king of Judah began to reign.* **2** *Ahaz was twenty years old when he became king, and he reigned in Jerusalem sixteen years. Unlike David his father, he did not do what was right in the eyes of the LORD his God.* **3** *He walked in the ways of the kings of Israel and even sacrificed his son in the fire, following the detestable ways of the nations the LORD had driven out before the Israelites.* **4** *He offered sacrifices and burned incense at the high places, on the hilltops and under every spreading tree.* **5** *Then Rezin king of Aram and Pekah son of Remaliah king of Israel marched up to fight against Jerusalem and besieged Ahaz, but they could not overpower him.* **6** *At that time, Rezin king of Aram recovered Elath for Aram by driving out the men of Judah. Edomites then moved into Elath and have lived there to this day.* **7** *Ahaz sent messengers to say to Tiglath-Pileser king of Assyria, "I am your servant and vassal. Come up and save me out of the hand of the king of Aram and of the king of Israel, who are attacking me."* **8** *And Ahaz took the silver and gold found in the temple of the LORD and in the treasuries of the royal palace and sent it as a gift to the king of Assyria.* **9** *The king of Assyria complied by attacking Damascus and capturing it. He deported its inhabitants to Kir and put Rezin to death.*

2 Kings 17:1-6
***1** In the twelfth year of Ahaz king of Judah, Hoshea son of Elah became king of Israel in Samaria, and he reigned nine years.*
***2** He did evil in the eyes of the LORD, but not like the kings of Israel who preceded him. **3** Shalmaneser king of Assyria came up to attack Hoshea, who had been Shalmaneser's vassal and had paid him tribute. **4** But the king of Assyria discovered that Hoshea was a traitor, for he had sent envoys to So king of Egypt, and he no longer paid tribute to the king of Assyria, as he had done year by year. Therefore Shalmaneser seized him and put him in prison. **5** The king of Assyria invaded the entire land, marched against Samaria and laid siege to it for three years. **6** In the ninth year of Hoshea, the king of Assyria captured Samaria and deported the Israelites to Assyria. He settled them in Halah, in Gozan on the Habor River and in the towns of the Medes.*

For Judah, the 2 Southern tribes

Isaiah 7:17-25
***17** The LORD will bring on you [Ahaz, king of Judah] and on your people and on the house of your father a time unlike any since Ephraim broke away from Judah--he will bring the king of Assyria." **18** In that day the LORD will whistle for flies from the distant streams of Egypt and for bees from the land of Assyria.*
19** They will all come and settle in the steep ravines and in the crevices in the rocks, on all the thornbushes and at all the water holes. **20** In that day the Lord will use a razor hired from beyond the River--the king of Assyria--to shave your head and the hair of your legs, and to take off your beards also. **21** In that day, a man will keep alive a young cow and two goats. **22** And because of the abundance of the milk they give, he will have curds to eat. All who remain in the land will eat curds and honey. **23
*In that day, in every place where there were a thousand vines worth a thousand silver shekels, there will be only briers and thorns. **24** Men will go there with bow and arrow, for the land*

will be covered with briers and thorns. **25** *As for all the hills*
once cultivated by the hoe, you will no longer go there for fear of
the briers and thorns; they will become places where cattle are
turned loose and where sheep run.

Isaiah 8:4-8
4 *Before the boy knows how to say 'My father' or 'My mother,'*
the wealth of Damascus and the plunder of Samaria will be car-
ried off by the king of Assyria." **5** *The LORD spoke to me again:*
6 *"Because this people has rejected the gently flowing waters of*
Shiloah and rejoices over Rezin and the son of Remaliah, **7** *there-*
fore the Lord is about to bring against them the mighty floodwa-
ters of the River-- the king of Assyria with all his pomp. It will
overflow all its channels, run over all its banks **8** *and sweep on*
into Judah, swirling over it, passing through it and reaching up
to the neck. Its outspread wings will cover the breadth of your
land, O Immanuel!"

2 Kings 18:13-16
13 *In the fourteenth year of King Hezekiah's reign, Sennacherib*
king of Assyria attacked all the fortified cities of Judah and cap-
tured them. **14** *So Hezekiah king of Judah sent this message to*
the king of Assyria at Lachish: "I have done wrong. Withdraw
from me, and I will pay whatever you demand of me." The king
of Assyria exacted from Hezekiah king of Judah three hundred
talents of silver and thirty talents of gold. **15** *So Hezekiah gave*
him all the silver that was found in the temple of the LORD and
in the treasuries of the royal palace. **16** *At this time Hezekiah*
king of Judah stripped off the gold with which he had covered
the doors and doorposts of the temple of the LORD, and gave it
to the king of Assyria.

2 Kings 18:17-25
17 *The king of Assyria sent his supreme commander, his chief*
officer and his field commander with a large army, from Lachish

to King Hezekiah at Jerusalem. They came up to Jerusalem and stopped at the aqueduct of the Upper Pool, on the road to the Washerman's Field. ***18*** *They called for the king; and Eliakim son of Hilkiah the palace administrator, Shebna the secretary, and Joah son of Asaph the recorder went out to them.* ***19*** *The field commander said to them, "Tell Hezekiah: " 'This is what the great king, the king of Assyria, says: On what are you basing this confidence of yours?* ***20*** *You say you have strategy and military strength--but you speak only empty words. On whom are you depending, that you rebel against me?* ***21*** *Look now, you are depending on Egypt, that splintered reed of a staff, which pierces a man's hand and wounds him if he leans on it! Such is Pharaoh king of Egypt to all who depend on him.* ***22*** *And if you say to me, "We are depending on the LORD our God"--isn't he the one whose high places and altars Hezekiah removed, saying to Judah and Jerusalem, "You must worship before this altar in Jerusalem"?* ***23*** *" 'Come now, make a bargain with my master, the king of Assyria: I will give you two thousand horses--if you can put riders on them!* ***24*** *How can you repulse one officer of the least of my master's officials, even though you are depending on Egypt for chariots and horsemen?* ***25*** *Furthermore, have I come to attack and destroy this place without word from the LORD? The LORD himself told me to march against this country and destroy it.' "*

Isaiah 10:5-15

5 *"Woe to the Assyrian, the rod of my anger, in whose hand is the club of my wrath!* ***6*** *I send him against a godless nation, I dispatch him against a people who anger me, to seize loot and snatch plunder, and to trample them down like mud in the streets.* ***7*** *But this is not what he intends, this is not what he has in mind; his purpose is to destroy, to put an end to many nations.* ***8*** *'Are not my commanders all kings?' he says.* ***9*** *'Has not Calno fared like Carchemish? Is not Hamath like Arpad, and Samaria like Damascus?* ***10*** *As my hand seized the kingdoms of* *the idols, kingdoms whose images excelled those of Jerusalem and Samaria--* ***11*** *shall I not deal with Jerusalem and her images as I dealt with Samaria and her idols?' "* ***12*** *When the Lord has finished all his work against Mount Zion and Jerusalem, he will say, "I will punish the king of Assyria for the willful pride of his heart and the haughty look in his eyes.* ***13*** *For he says: " 'By the strength of my hand I have done this, and by my wisdom, because I have understanding. I removed the boundaries of nations, I plundered their treasures; like a mighty one I subdued their kings.* ***14*** *As one reaches into a nest, so my hand reached for the wealth of the nations; as men gather abandoned eggs, so I gathered all the countries; not one flapped a wing, or opened its mouth to chirp.' "* ***15*** *Does the ax raise itself above him who swings it, or the saw boast against him who uses it? As if a rod were to wield him who lifts it up, or a club brandish him who is not wood!*

2 Kings 19:35-36
35 *That night the angel of the LORD went out and put to death a hundred and eighty-five thousand men in the Assyrian camp. When the people got up the next morning--there were all the dead bodies!* ***36*** *So Sennacherib king of Assyria broke camp and withdrew. He returned to Nineveh and stayed there.*

2 Kings 20:12-18
12 *At that time Merodach-Baladan son of Baladan king of Babylon sent Hezekiah letters and a gift, because he had heard of Hezekiah's illness.* ***13*** *Hezekiah received the messengers and showed them all that was in his storehouses--the silver, the gold, the spices and the fine oil--his armory and everything found among his treasures. There was nothing in his palace or in all his kingdom that Hezekiah did not show them.* ***14*** *Then Isaiah the prophet went to King Hezekiah and asked, "What did those men say, and where did they come from?" "From a distant land," Hezekiah replied. "They came from Babylon."* ***15***

*The prophet asked, "What did they see in your palace?" "They
saw everything in my palace," Hezekiah said. "There is nothing
among my treasures that I did not show them."* ***16*** *Then Isaiah
said to Hezekiah, "Hear the word of the LORD:* ***17*** *The time
will surely come when everything in your palace, and all that
your fathers have stored up until this day, will be carried off to
Babylon. Nothing will be left, says the LORD.* ***18*** *And some of
your descendants, your own flesh and blood that will be born
to you, will be taken away, and they will become eunuchs in the
palace of the king of Babylon."*

Habakkuk 1:5-11

5 *"Look at the nations and watch-- and be utterly amazed. For
I am going to do something in your days that you would not
believe, even if you were told.* ***6*** *I am raising up the Babylonians,
that ruthless and impetuous people, who sweep across the whole
earth to seize dwelling places not their own.* ***7*** *They are a feared
and dreaded people; they are a law to themselves and promote
their own honor.* ***8*** *Their horses are swifter than leopards, fiercer
than wolves at dusk. Their cavalry gallops headlong; their
horsemen come from afar. They fly like a vulture swooping to
devour;* ***9*** *they all come bent on violence. Their hordes advance
like a desert wind and gather prisoners like sand.* ***10*** *They
deride kings and scoff at rulers. They laugh at all fortified cities;
they build earthen ramps and capture them.* ***11*** *Then they sweep
past like the wind and go on-- guilty men, whose own strength
is their god."*

Jeremiah 5:18-19

18 *"Yet even in those days," declares the LORD, "I will not
destroy you completely.* ***19*** *And when the people ask, 'Why has
the LORD our God done all this to us?' you will tell them, 'As
you have forsaken me and served foreign gods in your own land,
so now you will serve foreigners in a land not your own.'*

2 Kings 24:1-2
***1** During Jehoiakim's reign, Nebuchadnezzar king of Babylon invaded the land, and Jehoiakim became his vassal for three years. But then he changed his mind and rebelled against Nebuchadnezzar. **2** The LORD sent Babylonian, Aramean, Moabite and Ammonite raiders against him. He sent them to destroy Judah, in accordance with the word of the LORD proclaimed by his servants the prophets.*

2 Kings 24:8-17
***8** Jehoiachin was eighteen years old when he became king, and he reigned in Jerusalem three months. His mother's name was Nehushta daughter of Elnathan; she was from Jerusalem.*
***9** He did evil in the eyes of the LORD, just as his father had*
*done. **10** At that time the officers of Nebuchadnezzar king of*
*Babylon advanced on Jerusalem and laid siege to it, **11** and*
Nebuchadnezzar himself came up to the city while his officers
*were besieging it. **12** Jehoiachin king of Judah, his mother, his attendants, his nobles and his officials all surrendered to him. In the eighth year of the reign of the king of Babylon,*
*he took Jehoiachin prisoner. **13** As the LORD had declared,*
Nebuchadnezzar removed all the treasures from the temple of the LORD and from the royal palace, and took away all the gold articles that Solomon king of Israel had made for the temple
*of the LORD. **14** He carried into exile all Jerusalem: all the officers and fighting men, and all the craftsmen and artisans--a total of ten thousand. Only the poorest people of the land were*
*left. **15** Nebuchadnezzar took Jehoiachin captive to Babylon. He also took from Jerusalem to Babylon the king's mother, his*
*wives, his officials and the leading men of the land. **16** The king*
of Babylon also deported to Babylon the entire force of seven thousand fighting men, strong and fit for war, and a thousand
*craftsmen and artisans. **17** He made Mattaniah, Jehoiachin's*
uncle, king in his place and changed his name to Zedekiah.

2 Kings 25:1-21
1 So in the ninth year of Zedekiah's reign, on the tenth day of the
tenth month, Nebuchadnezzar king of Babylon marched against
Jerusalem with his whole army. He encamped outside the city
and built siege works all around it. **2** The city was kept under
siege until the eleventh year of King Zedekiah. **3** By the ninth
day of the [fourth] month the famine in the city had become so
severe that there was no food for the people to eat. **4** Then the
city wall was broken through, and the whole army fled at night
through the gate between the two walls near the king's garden,
though the Babylonians were surrounding the city. They fled
toward the Arabah, **5** but the Babylonian army pursued the king
and overtook him in the plains of Jericho. All his soldiers were
separated from him and scattered, **6** and he was captured. He
was taken to the king of Babylon at Riblah, where sentence was
pronounced on him. **7** They killed the sons of Zedekiah before
his eyes. Then they put out his eyes, bound him with bronze
shackles and took him to Babylon. **8** On the seventh day of the
fifth month, in the nineteenth year of Nebuchadnezzar king of
Babylon, Nebuzaradan commander of the imperial guard, an
official of the king of Babylon, came to Jerusalem. **9** He set fire
to the temple of the LORD, the royal palace and all the houses
of Jerusalem. Every important building he burned down. **10** The
whole Babylonian army, under the commander of the imperial
guard, broke down the walls around Jerusalem. **11** Nebuzaradan
the commander of the guard carried into exile the people who
remained in the city, along with the rest of the populace and
those who had gone over to the king of Babylon. **12** But the commander left behind some of the poorest people of the land to work
the vineyards and fields. **13** The Babylonians broke up the bronze
pillars, the movable stands and the bronze Sea that were at the
temple of the LORD and they carried the bronze to Babylon. **14**
They also took away the pots, shovels, wick trimmers, dishes
and all the bronze articles used in the temple service. **15** The
commander of the imperial guard took away the censers and

sprinkling bowls--all that were made of pure gold or silver. ***16***
The bronze from the two pillars, the Sea and the movable stands,
which Solomon had made for the temple of the LORD, was more
than could be weighed. ***17*** *Each pillar was twenty-seven feet*
high. The bronze capital on top of one pillar was four and a half
feet high and was decorated with a network and pomegranates
of bronze all around. The other pillar, with its network, was sim-
ilar. ***18*** *The commander of the guard took as prisoners Seraiah*
the chief priest, Zephaniah the priest next in rank and the three
doorkeepers. ***19*** *Of those still in the city, he took the officer in*
charge of the fighting men and five royal advisers. He also took
the secretary who was chief officer in charge of conscripting the
people of the land and sixty of his men who were found in the
city. ***20*** *Nebuzaradan the commander took them all and brought*
them to the king of Babylon at Riblah. ***21*** *There at Riblah, in the*
land of Hamath, the king had them executed. So Judah went into
captivity, away from her land.

GOD'S RESPONSES TO GREED

James 4:1-6

1 *What causes fights and quarrels among you? Don't they come from your desires that battle within you?* **2 You want something but don't get it**. *You kill and covet, but you cannot have what you want. You quarrel and fight. You do not have, because you do not ask God.* **3 When you ask, you do not receive, because you ask with wrong motives, that you may spend what you get on your pleasures.** 4 **You adulterous people, don't you know that friendship with the world is hatred toward God? Anyone who chooses to be a friend of the world becomes an enemy of God. 5 Or do you think Scripture says without reason that the spirit he caused to live in us envies intensely?** 6 **But he gives us more grace. That is why Scripture says: "God opposes the proud but gives grace to the humble."**

2 Peter 1:16-21

16 *We did not follow cleverly invented stories when we told you about the power and coming of our Lord Jesus Christ, but we were eyewitnesses of his majesty.* **17** *For he received honor and glory from God the Father when the voice came to him from the Majestic Glory, saying, "This is my Son, whom I love; with him I am well pleased."* **18** *We ourselves heard this voice that came from heaven when we were with him on the sacred mountain.* **19** *And we have the* **word of the prophets [note these are the**

OT prophets] *made more certain, and* ***you will do well to pay attention to it****, as to a light shining in a dark place, until the day dawns and the morning star rises in your hearts.* ***20*** *Above all, you must understand that no prophecy of Scripture came about by the prophet's own interpretation.* ***21*** *For prophecy never had its origin in the will of man, but men spoke from God as they were carried along by the Holy Spirit.*

Colossians 3:5-7
5 *Put to death, therefore, whatever belongs to your earthly nature: sexual immorality, impurity, lust, evil desires* ***and greed, which is idolatry.*** *6* ***Because of these, the wrath of God is coming****. 7 You used to walk in these ways, in the life you once lived.*

Ephesians 5:5-6
5 *For of this you can be sure: No immoral, impure or* ***greedy person--such a man is an idolater****--has any inheritance in the kingdom of Christ and of God.* ***6*** *Let no one deceive you with empty words, for* ***because of such things God's wrath comes on those who are disobedient****.*

Romans 11:13-24
13 *I am talking to you Gentiles [note: this is the Gentile church compared to Israel], not an individual]. Inasmuch as I am the apostle to the Gentiles, I make much of my ministry* ***14*** *in the hope that I may somehow arouse my own people to envy and save some of them.* ***15*** *For if their rejection is the reconciliation of the world, what will their acceptance be but life from the dead?* ***16***
If the part of the dough offered as firstfruits is holy, then the whole batch is holy; if the root is holy, so are the branches. ***17***
If some of the branches have been broken off, and you, though a wild olive shoot, have been grafted in among the others and now share in the nourishing sap from the olive root, ***18 do not boast over those branches****. If you do, consider this: You do not support the root, but the root supports you.* ***19*** *You will say then,*

"Branches were broken off so that I could be grafted in." **20**
Granted. But they were broken off because of unbelief, and
you stand by faith. Do not be arrogant, but be afraid. *21* ***For if***
God did not spare the natural branches, he will not spare you
either. **22** *Consider therefore the kindness and sternness of God:*
sternness to those who fell, but kindness to you, provided that
you continue in his kindness. ***Otherwise, you also will be cut off.***
23 *And if they do not persist in unbelief, they will be grafted in,*
for God is able to graft them in again. **24** *After all, if you were*
cut out of an olive tree that is wild by nature, and contrary to
nature were grafted into a cultivated olive tree, how much more
readily will these, the natural branches, be grafted into their
own olive tree!

WHAT THEN SHOULD WE DO?

The list could be long, but here are some suggestions. These were essential in the days of Judah and the city of Jerusalem where the temple was. The relevance is that under the New Covenant, the Jerusalem that is above is our mother (*Galatians 4:26)* and our body is the temple of the Holy Spirit (*1 Corinthians 6:19; Ephesians 2:19-22).*

Zephaniah 2:3 [of Judah]
3 Seek the LORD, all you humble of the land, you who do what he commands. ***Seek righteousness, seek humility****; perhaps you will be sheltered on the day of the LORD's anger*

Ezekiel 9:3-4 [of Jerusalem and the temple]
3 Now the glory of the God of Israel went up from above the cherubim, where it had been, and moved to the threshold of the temple. Then the LORD called to the man clothed in linen who had the writing kit at his side 4 and said to him, "Go throughout the city of Jerusalem and put a mark on the foreheads of those who ***grieve and lament*** *over all the detestable things* [cf., idolatry in the temple that provokes the Lord's jealousy, see *Ezekiel* chapter 8] *that are done in it."*

CPSIA information can be obtained at www.ICGtesting.com
Printed in the USA
LVOW06s0100220714

395371LV00001B/1/P